"This collection of spiritual refreshing and hope-filled contrast to the hysterical and near-apocalyptic tone of most contemporary reflections on life in the age of COVID-19. To perceive the workings of a merciful God in the midst of adversity has always been prized as the sign of a true Christian contemplative: in these essays, the reader is invited to share the fruit of Pastor Thomas's contemplative gift."

—LUKE DYSINGER,
OSB, Saint John's Seminary

"Pastor Thomas has a lovely way of expressing God's grace and love in a warm, accessible, and authentic way. In each essay, he invites us to be more faithful and grounded as we see and experience life in all of its complexities. While the pandemic will one day be over, this book will continue to provide wisdom and good news to those who read it."

—SHELLEY BRYAN WEE,
Bishop, Northwest Washington Synod, ELCA

"Throughout the early months of the COVID-19 pandemic, I hungered for words to help me cope and thrive in spite of sheltering in place. Pastor Thomas's weekly letters to his congregation connected the Scriptures, contemporary writers, and personal experiences with everyday feelings of loss, powerlessness, and self-pity. This devotional is timeless with encouraging messages of hope, faith, and love."

—LOUISE EVENSON,
retired Educator

"Christian leaders and congregations will highly benefit from *Lily Packed a Facemask*. . . . With his intellectual agility, his ability to draw from years of shepherding church congregations, and his sense of humor, Thomas offers the family of believers a lifeboat to navigate the sea of confusion and debilitating chaos caused by the COVID-19 pandemic."

—NYAMUTERA JOSEPH,
Founder and Director, Rabagirana Ministries

"Larry Thomas looks upon the world with 'the eyes of (his) heart enlightened" (Eph 1:18), seeing in the ordinary the extraordinary presence of divine grace. In *Lily Packed a Facemask*, he writes with simple clarity and gentle joy as he shares his vision of God in our midst even as we lived through a pandemic together. This book comes out of a specific time, but it shares timeless wisdom."

—DELMER CHILTON,
author of *The Gospel According to Aunt Mildred: Stories of Family and Faith*

Lily Packed a Facemask

Lily Packed a Facemask

Pastoral Letters During a Pandemic

Larry E. Thomas

Foreword by Carl Wilkens

RESOURCE *Publications* · Eugene, Oregon

LILY PACKED A FACEMASK
Pastoral Letters During a Pandemic

Resource Publications
An Imprint of Wipf and Stock Publishers
199 W. 8th Ave., Suite 3
Eugene, OR 97401

www.wipfandstock.com

PAPERBACK ISBN: 978-1-6667-1330-5
HARDCOVER ISBN: 978-1-6667-1331-2
EBOOK ISBN: 978-1-6667-1332-9

.   NOVEMBER 8, 2021 9:14 AM

For Ann. Always.

Although I have much to write to you, I would rather not use paper and ink; instead I hope to come to you and talk with you face to face, so that our joy may be complete.

(2 JOHN 12)

Contents

LILY PACKED A FACEMASK
PASTORAL LETTERS DURING A PANDEMIC

Permissions

Wendell Berry, "The Peace of Wild Things," from *New Collected Poems*, Copyright © 2012 by Wendell Berry. Reprinted with the permission of The Permissions Company, LLC on behalf of Counterpoint Press, counterpointpress.com.

Bruce Beresford, Director. 1983. *Tender Mercies*. Screenplay by Horton Foote. Copyright © EMI Films. Reprinted with permission of ICM Partners.

Michael Kelly Blanchard, "Be Ye Glad." Copyright ©1980 Quail Ministries Inc./Gotz Music Inc. Used by permission.

Braver Angels, "With Malice Toward None Pledge." Copyright © 2020, Braver Angels. Used by permission.

Frederick Buechner, *Beyond Words*. Copyright © 2004 by Frederick Buechner. Used by permission of HarperCollins Publishers.

Frederick Buechner, *Wishful Thinking*. Copyright © 1973 by Frederick Buechner. Used by permission by HarperCollins Publishers.

Frederick Dale Bruner, *Matthew, A Commentary, Volume 1*. Copyright © 2004 by Wm. B. Eerdmans Publishing Company. Reprinted with permission by Wm. B. Eerdmans Publishing Company.

Joan Chittister, *The Rule of Benedict: Insights For The Ages*. Copyright © 1992 by Joan D. Chirrister, O.S.B. All rights reserved. Used by permission of The Crossroad Publishing Company,

Foreword

IT'S ALWAYS SUCH A PLEASURE to introduce my "got your back" friend Larry Thomas. Larry is one of my favorite people to brainstorm with! Not only is he upbeat and optimistic, but he's so well-read. He has this uncanny ability to reach inside his memory and grab an example or a relevant guiding principle to give direction and shape to whatever we are working on.

Speaking of relevant, that's one of the top qualities I've found in this book, which is brimming with what I call "centering sessions." Each chapter has a tool like the "Mercy Rule," or an inspiring new idea such as God whispering in our ear, "Surprise me." I'd invite you to dig into these chapters looking for the relevant values, tools, and for the morsels of inspiration they contain. The intentionality of this practice paid off for me with the morning's stories and lessons re-centering me throughout the day and grounding me deeper in the core value or theme of that chapter.

Another thing that took me by surprise was that while I loved starting my day with these letters, I also found myself picking the book up again as my head hit the pillow—a centering, as it were, before sleep.

Larry's writing of these letters to his parishioners was very much in response to the daily—and sometimes seemingly impossible—challenges of the ever-changing realities of life during the COVID-19 pandemic. Having said that, as I've read and reread the letters, I found timeless wisdom and application in them. I think this is at least partially due to Larry's generous weaving in and out of the ideas and quotes from other writers along with his own words. I mentioned earlier that Larry has read widely; fortunately for us readers, Larry's writing flows seamlessly between his own thoughts, experiences, and strategies, and the thoughts, experiences, and strategies of world-class writers. I often found myself going off to the Internet to learn more about the writers who have had such a marvelous impact on Larry's journey. I'm super grateful for so many wonderful new "literary friends."

Lastly, I want to share how many times I caught myself smiling at Larry's candor and vulnerability. I think we are all tempted, at times, to cast ourselves in a favorable light; I know I am. That's why I so appreciated Larry's honesty and openness as I traveled through this book. The authenticity and relatability of his journey came through in heaping portions that I found delightful and encouraging.

As Larry writes later on in this book, I witnessed the 100 days of genocide in Rwanda against the Tutsi in 1994, something that could destroy a person's soul—or, conversely, drive us deeper into the arms the Shepherd that David describes in Ps 23. I see the fingerprints of our divine Shepherd all over the pages of this book and trust that you will be blessed again and again— just as I was each time I picked it up!

Carl Wilkens
Cofounder and Director
World Outside My Shoes

Preface

ON FEBRUARY 27, 2020—THE DAY after Ash Wednesday—my wife Ann and I left our home in Issaquah, Washington for a three-week trip to visit family in Colorado and Texas. We assumed that when we returned from our travels, I would be working in my office at Sammamish Hills Lutheran Church, just a short drive from home. Turns out, when I went back to work it was from a makeshift office in a bedroom in Flower Mound, Texas.

During our trip, the world had changed.

In order to be of service to the congregation in Washington, while sheltering in place in Texas, I began to write pastoral letters that would be emailed to the congregation twice a week. My purpose in writing these letters was to reflect on the experience of striving to be people of faith, hope, and love, in the midst of a pandemic and all of its collateral impacts.

Over the course of the year, the challenges of the pandemic were compounded by record unemployment, economic uncertainty, a deepening divide among the electorate, social unrest in the aftermath of the killing of George Floyd, wildfires in the West, hurricanes in the Southeast, national, statewide and local elections, and hundreds of thousands of our fellow citizens dying from COVID-19.

I am grateful for your interest in *Lily Packed a Facemask: Pastoral Letters During a Pandemic*. My hope is that these letters will help, some.

Larry E. Thomas
Issaquah, Washington

Acknowledgements

My parents Kenneth and Janice Thomas introduced my sister Gloria and me to the good news of Jesus Christ and the wonderful world of reading. Honestly, I can't remember which came first. The first "real" book my mother read to me was *The Lion, The Witch and The Wardrobe: A Story for Children* by C.S. Lewis. My worn and tattered copy sits on a bookshelf in an antique secretary just above the shelf that holds my first Bible. My parents' love for Jesus and books was contagious. I can't imagine my life without books or Jesus.

Ann Thomas is someone else I can't imagine living my life without. Thanks to Ann, my beloved spouse of fifty-one years, for personifying the grace and love of God. Daily. My constant companion during the pandemic, Ann was the first reader of these letters and served as encourager, editor, consultant, and truth teller.

I'm grateful to Delmer Chilton and Carl Wilkens for their timely and thoughtful notes on many of these letters. Thanks to Managing Editor Matt Wimer of Wipf and Stock Publishers for his support and to Tim Hoiland, who copy-edited the manuscript.

It was a blessing to serve Sammamish Hills Lutheran Church, for two years and four months. My gratitude to the members, friends, and staff of SHLC is boundless. Special thanks to my 2020 SHLC co-workers: Alison Carpenter, Carol Churchill, Eric Hanson, Becky Kleinknecht, Sungjoon Lee, Kristine Meyer, Anna Morris, Aleta Pritchard, Philip Reitz, Robin Shealy, Jessica Stan, Susan Wolbrecht, and Stan Adams, church council president.

Acknowledgements

I dedicate this collection of pastoral letters to our family: Anders, Megan, Soren, Rebecca, Stephan, Beya, Enzo, Emily, Dontay, Lily and Ashton. Of all the people I missed during the pandemic's social isolation and sheltering in place, you are the ones I missed the most.

Love in Action

March 27, 2020

Let us love not in word or speech, but in truth and
action. (1 John 3:18)

YESTERDAY, ANN AND I MET Reggie the notary. He came to our
temporary home in Flower Mound, Texas (just north of Dallas)
to notarize some papers for us that needed signing. Due to social distancing concerns we decided to meet Reggie in the garage.
We set up a couple of chairs and a card table and sanitized them.
Reggie was kind, gracious, and appreciative of our efforts to keep
our distance, and be safe, as we took care of business.

Over the course of our brief meeting, we talked about the
impacts of the coronavirus outbreak. Reggie's father is a pastor
of a church outside of Dallas who has continued to lead Sunday
morning worship services despite the pandemic. Reggie told us
that even though he's the son, this week he told his father, that for
the sake of the well- being of the congregation and their neighbors
his father had to stop leading Sunday morning worship services.
His father agreed.

The more I think about the current state of affairs the more
grateful I am for people who are doing their best to follow the di-
rectives of public servants to shelter in place and practice social
distancing. After all, social distancing isn't anti-social; it's an act of

self-denial and sacrificial love for the sake of our neighbors. (It's also known as the Golden Rule.) The hard truth is that it's just not about me; it's about public health and safety, it's about you and your neighbors and our mutual wellbeing. Social distancing and staying in place are what love in action looks like in the current moment.

Over a hundred years ago, the Salvation Army was holding its annual convention. The group's founder, Gen. William Booth, could not attend so he cabled the convention his message. It consisted of one word: "Others." If there's one word for the living of these days, it's others. This is not easy; I'm hardwired for "me" but I know that for the time being, loving others, praying for others, emailing others, texting and/or phoning others, checking in with others, and staying connected with others is the way to go. (Now that I think about it, as disciples and apprentices to Jesus, is there really any time when "others" isn't the way to go, the way to live and the way to love?)

God is Our Refuge and Strength

March 31, 2020

God is our refuge and strength, a very present help in
trouble. Therefore we will not fear, though the earth
should change, though the mountains shake in the heart
of the sea, though its waters roar and foam, though the
mountains tremble with its tumult. (Ps 46:1–3)

It's Monday and we're sheltering in place in Flower Mound,
Texas. Most days we go for walks; once or twice a week I get out
and go to the local supermarket. Tomorrow I'll drive our daughter
Emily to her weekly appointment with her obstetrician. (Her baby
is due in April.) Otherwise, we're sheltering in place. Just like you.

It's been just over two weeks since the coronavirus outbreak
began to impact my movements. Two weeks ago today, I was at
a local coffee shop, enjoying a mocha and writing a letter to you.
Later that week the shop closed its doors and started serving coffee
curbside. I'm happy to report that (so far) I'm not going stir crazy.
I am and we are managing just fine. I'm grateful for the technology
that helps us stay in touch: smart phones, computers, Facebook
and Zoom.

What I'm learning is that sheltering in place and social distancing is taxing. It takes a toll. I was talking about this with a

friend last night. The mental, emotional, and spiritual energy required to cope with the impacts of the coronavirus pandemic together with the constant news feed seem to exacerbate the challenges and stresses of daily life. It's harder to get through the day.

I'm increasingly aware that even under normal circumstances I sometimes *react* rather than *respond* to stress; nowadays I find myself sometimes *overreacting* to people and to situations as if I lack the capacity to handle more stress. That's not how I want to live, no matter what's going on inside (my heart or our shelter) let alone what's happening outside—around the block and around the world.

Another thing I'm learning: I need to remember to grieve. I have a friend who is hospitalized and waiting to hear if he has COVID-19. As of Saturday, March 28, 2020, there were 4,896 confirmed cases of COVID-19 in the state of Washington and 169 confirmed deaths. I mourn this loss of life and grieve for the survivors. Some days the bad news feels like it's more than we can bear: the sickness, deaths, shortages, and impacts on the economy can all overwhelm us.

There are other losses too: the loss of ordinary-taken-for-granted freedoms like our mobility or meeting up with friends for coffee, a beer, or a meal. Added together with missed this and postponed that plus all manner of cancellations and you get even more loss. Some of these are small losses to be sure, but they are losses nonetheless.

When I'm tempted to sheltering in place self-pity, I remember my Rwandan friend Theo Mushinzimana as well as Immaculee Illibagiza, the author of *Left to Tell: Discovering God Amidst the Rwandan Holocaust*. During the 1994 Rwandan genocide against the Tutsi, Ms. Illibagiza spent 91 days with seven other women huddled together in the cramped bathroom of a local pastor's home hiding from genocidaires. Ninety-one days. My friend Theo Mushinzima spent most of the genocide—which lasted about100 days— hiding in a garbage pit under banana leaves or under the roof of a house (If that's not sheltering in place, I don't know what is.) Anywhere from eight hundred thousand to one million people were slaughtered during the genocide. I could learn a thing or two about patience and perseverance from Ms. Illibagiza and Mr. Mushinzimana.

The words of Psalm 46 are words of comfort and hope. Always. The psalmist's words remind me that God is with us even when the world feels like it is spinning out of control. God is our refuge and our strength; our shelter from the storm, no matter what. Fearless, thanks to God's faithfulness, we make our way through these days of social distancing and sheltering in place trusting that God holds each one of us in the palm of God's hand, promising to never leave us or forsake us. In an email to some friends today, Ann wrote these words: "Our vacation-turned sojourn finds us settled in with Emily, Dontay, and Lily in Texas. We're awaiting the new baby's birth, hoping she will shelter in place in Emily for at least two more weeks."

Our Texas family is sheltering in place waiting for new life. Together with you, we're waiting for this surreal season to give way to new life abounding. One day at a time, we're staying the course and trusting God's faithfulness.

Hand Washing and Holy Week

April 3, 2020

When Pilate saw that he could do nothing (to spare the
life of Jesus) but rather that a riot was beginning, he took
some water and washed his hands before the crowd, saying,
"I am innocent of this man's blood; see to it yourselves."
(Matt 27:24)

During a global pandemic, one of the cheapest, easiest,
and most important ways to prevent the spread of a virus
is to wash your hands frequently with soap and water.
(The UNICEF website)

WE ARE AWASH IN HAND washing. It's Friday morning and I'm sitting at the kitchen table as Lily, our four-year old granddaughter, washes her hands and sings "Happy Birthday." This ritual, undertaken billions of times a day, around the globe, is one thing (together with sheltering in place and social distancing) we can do to stem the tide of the coronavirus outbreak. So, we wash our hands and some of us sing "Happy Birthday."

On Monday evening people from Sammamish Hills Lutheran Church and Mt. Si Lutheran Church in North Bend, Washington, gathered online to record a group reading of the Passion according to St. Matthew in preparation for the Palm Sunday online worship service. After an early miscue (courtesy of yours truly) we recorded the reading in one take.

I've participated in lots of Palm Sunday readings of the Passion of our Lord over the years. Other than possible technical glitches or missed cues, I didn't expect anything out of the ordinary last Monday night (other than the extra-ordinary fact that isolated in our separate homes, we were pre-recording a group reading of the Passion according to St. Matthew for an *online* Palm Sunday worship service!)

The big surprise came when the narrator read the words, "When Pilate saw that he could do nothing (to spare the life of Jesus) he took some water and washed his hands."

Pilate washing his hands of any and all responsibility for the death of Jesus hit me like a bolt out of the blue. I flashed on the countless times a day I am and we are washing (or sanitizing) our hands hoping to prevent or slow the spread of the coronavirus. No big metaphors here; just practicing personal hygiene for the sake of ourselves and our neighbors.

Pilate's hand washing is a different matter altogether. Pilate washed his hands as a public act to absolve himself of any and all guilt for the death of Jesus. The most powerful man in town felt powerless to help Jesus in the face of the pressure of the religious leaders and their orchestrated public outcry for the release of Barabbas and the crucifixion of Jesus. In spite of his ceremonial washing, he was as guilty as sin, just like the rest of us.

In St. John's narrative of the Maundy Thursday Passover gathering (John 13:6–9) Jesus washes his disciples' feet as an example of sacrificial servant love that he prays they will offer each other. As he begins to wash Simon Peter's feet, Peter asks Jesus, "Lord, are you going to wash my feet?" Jesus replies, "You do not know now what I am doing, but later you will understand." Peter tells Jesus he doesn't want him to wash his feet. When Jesus tells him, "Unless I wash you, you have no share in me, " Peter says, "Lord, not my feet only but also my hands and my head!"

Sin sick and fearing for his life, Peter will, that very night, deny knowing Jesus, in spite of his assurances to the contrary. After the crucifixion, after the Easter Sunday resurrection of our Lord, and after the Ascension, Peter—forgiven, free, and spirit- empowered—will preach on Pentecost saying, "Repent and be baptized every one of you in the name of Jesus Christ so that your sins may be forgiven, and you will receive the gift of the Holy Spirit. For the promise is for you, for your children and for all who are far away, everyone whom the Lord our God calls to him" (Acts 2:38–39).

In other words, get your sins washed away in the new life river of Jesus' tender mercies and saving grace. Baptized, forgiven, and set free, the Holy Spirit will teach you that all the promises of God have your name written on them. In his letter to the Romans, St. Paul explains the wonder-working power of being washed in waters of baptism: "Do you not know that all of us who have been baptized into Christ Jesus were baptized into his death? Therefore we have been buried with him by baptism into death, so that, just as Christ was raised from the dead by the glory of the Father, so too we might walk in newness of life" (Rom 6:3–4).

Earlier this week I started counting how many times I washed my hands in one day. I can't remember if I lost count or threw in the towel but I know it seemed like every time I turned around I was washing my hands. I've been thinking about hand washing and Holy Week and wondering about turning this simple act into a redemptive ritual. Instead of singing "Happy Birthday," I'm going to write out this passage from Romans and tape it to the mirror above the sink and start memorizing it. The heart of what I want to remember about Holy Week and Easter is summed up in the grace-filled assurance of St. Peter's and St. Paul's words and the promise of new life: here, now, today.

A Cup of Hope

April 7, 2020

> Now may our Lord Jesus Christ himself, and God
> our Father, who loved us and through grace gave us
> eternal comfort and good hope, comfort your hearts
> and strengthen them in every good work and word.
> (2 Thess 2:16–17)

MOST MORNINGS, WE TAKE A walk along the local greenbelt trails.
Here in North Texas, the trees are draped in lively shades of green
and the flowers are in full bloom. The birdsong is a winsome ac-
companiment to our daily conversations. We greet fellow walkers with a wave or a hushed "hello." The last couple of days we've
noticed more walkers wearing facemasks. Thankfully, an Issaquah
friend made facemasks for the whole household and they arrived
in yesterday's mail.

One feature of our daily walks, are chalk messages written out
on the trail in broad strokes with a firm hand. Today's messages
were a medley of admonitions and inspiration: "Wear a Mask,"
"Check on your neighbor," "Hope is on the move," "There's always
hope, "and "Who do you need to thank today?" I was heartened
by the "hopeful" chalk messages as I was thinking about writing

about hope today. I'm grateful for the anonymous scribe cheering us on during this sobering season.

Yesterday morning I wrote some notes for a pastoral letter on the challenges of staying in place but then thought the better of it. Enough already. All of us are living the daily realities of staying put and social distancing. We know how hard this is. What's more, we don't know how long it will last. I don't know about you, but some days my resilience wavers. It's Holy Week and I need some hope. I want to remember it won't always be like this. Maybe you need to remember that, too.

Believe it or not, the days are coming when we'll break free of sheltering in place and social distancing and meet up for Sunday worship, coffee and conversation, a leisurely meal, or a night on the town. That's not the half of it. According to the Revelation to St. John, new heaven and new earth days are coming when God will make God's home with us: "God himself will be with them; God will wipe every tear from their eyes. Death will be no more; mourning and crying and pain will be no more, for the first things have passed away" (Rev 21:3–4).

Maundy Thursday's invitation to love others as God in Christ has loved us, Good Friday's message of God's unconditional love and forgiveness, together with our Easter Sunday "He is Risen" new life proclamations, sow seeds of hope a plenty in the hearts of God's people. Nourished by the love of God and the tender mercies of Jesus through the means of grace: word, water, wine, bread and each other, we are set free to join creation's songs of praise.

Speaking of hope: Last month, while visiting family in Denver, Colorado, Ann and I made a pilgrimage to Estes Park in northern Colorado. We've been planning an August 2020 family reunion at YMCA of the Rockies for almost a year. Last month we drove up to check it out since we'd never been there. We fell in love with the place. The campus, the facilities, and the mountains filled us with gratitude and joy. We bought a couple of YMCA of the Rockies mugs in the gift shop. They aren't mementos of something we wanted to *remember*: they are signs of hope for something we're looking forward *to*.

A Cup of Hope

Each morning, I fill my cup of hope with coffee, hoping that we will gather with our family this summer—and, if not then, in August 2021. (Update: the reunion has been postponed again until August 2022. Hope abides.) Our family reunion hope is *penultimate*; it steadies my sometimes believing, sometimes doubting heart. Frederick Buechner helps me remember:

> For Christians, hope is *ultimately* in Christ. The hope that he really is what for centuries we have been claiming he is. The hope that despite the fact that sin and death still rule the world, he somehow conquered them. The hope that in him, and through him, all of us stand a chance of somehow conquering them too. The hope that at some unforeseeable time and in some unimaginable way, he will return with healing in his wings. [1]

Take a moment. Pour yourself a cup of your favorite beverage or a mug of your favorite brew and ponder what you're hoping for, what you're looking forward to; consider how the promises of Holy Week and Easter give you heart and sustain you in faith, hope and love for the living of your life both now and in the days ahead. One more thing: did I mention that on this morning's walk we crossed paths with a young man wearing a blue t-shirt with the word "Hope" printed on the front?

1. Buechner, *Beyond Words*, 160.

Be Ye Glad

April 10, 2020

May you be made strong with all the strength that comes with God's glorious power, and may you be prepared to endure everything with patience, while joyfully giving thanks to the Father, who has enabled you to share in the inheritance of the saints in the light. We have been rescued from the power of darkness and transferred into the kingdom of God's beloved Son, in whom we have redemption, the forgiveness of sins. (Col 1:1–13)

THIS SUNDAY WILL BE MY second time watching Easter Sunday worship online. The first time was Easter Sunday four years ago. Ann and I were out of state caring for family members who were counting on us to pitch in and help out. We decided that attending an Easter Sunday worship service was out of the question, so we sat on the couch and watched an online celebration of the Resurrection of our Lord on my laptop computer. It wasn't as good as being there, but it was better than nothing.

That Easter we watched an online worship service streaming from a sanctuary overflowing with people. *This* Easter, I'll be worshipping online with you as we watch Easter Sunday worship with Sammamish Hills and Mt. Si Lutheran Church worship leaders and musicians leading our Easter worship remotely from their respective homes. I expect we will be blessed by the music and the Easter message of new life and hope, even as we huddle at home, wishing we could be *together.*

This week I've been thinking about another Easter. At the time, I was the pastor of a congregation in Los Angeles, California. We were planning an Easter Sunday outdoor sunrise service followed by an indoor Easter celebration. The sunrise service got rained out so we ended up in the sanctuary. I can't remember if I planned on singing Michael Kelly Blanchard's "Be Ye Glad" solo acapella or if it was spontaneous. What I do remember was that it wasn't a great idea—I've been blessed with some skills and gifts but singing solo acapella isn't one of them. Honest.

I first learned about the music of Michael Kelly Blanchard in the summer of 1981. We attended a Peter, Paul and Mary concert and during his solo portion of the show, Noel Paul Stookey sang Mr. Blanchard's song, "Then The Quail Came," a beautiful, haunting, song about Moses' and Israel's wilderness wanderings and God's faithfulness.

A few days later I was in a local Bible bookstore checking out the record bin and found myself looking at "Love Lives On," a Michael Kelley Blanchard record. I bought it, took it home, put it on the turntable and was introduced to his wonderful and sublime songs of faith, hope, love, struggle, and real life. Ann wrote him a letter, he wrote back, and we've been friends with Michael ever since. "Be Ye Glad" was on that record.

I've been thinking about "Be Ye Glad," a lot lately. Maybe it's the line "in these days of confused situations, in these nights or a restless remorse" or the line "there is no disease or no struggle that can pull you from God, be ye glad." I looked up the lyrics and listened to it earlier this week. Mercy sakes! If "Be Ye Glad" isn't the perfect song for this coronavirus outbreak / Holy Week / Easter season, I don't know what is. [1]

Paraphrasing the words St. Paul prayed for his Colossian friends, I pray that you, friends in Christ, may be strengthened

1. Michael Kelly Blanchard, *Be Ye Glad.*

to endure everything with patience while joyfully giving thanks to the Father who has rescued us from the power of darkness and transferred into the kingdom of God's beloved Son, in whom we have redemption, the forgiveness of sins. This Good Friday, Holy Saturday, and Easter weekend, I'll be making time to listen to "Be Ye Glad." You can check out a version sung by Michael Kelly Blanchard and Noel Paul Stookey on YouTube.

Powerlessness, Prayer, and the Sufficiency of God's Grace

April 14, 2020

Three times I appealed to the Lord about this that it would leave me, but he said to me, "My grace is sufficient for you, for power is made perfect in weakness." (2 Cor 12:8–9b)

IT WAS A SUNDAY MORNING and my friend the Rev. Dr. Delmer Chilton and I were driving to Hayesville, North Carolina, to attend worship at the local Episcopal church. It was a crisp, spring morning and the sun was rising over the foothills. We came up over a rise and all of a sudden the windshield was covered in blazing sunlight. We couldn't see a thing. Delmer quickly pulled off the road, but not before we were rear-ended by a car which then hit another car. Miraculously, no one was injured.

I don't think I've never felt more powerless. Though the experience only lasted a few seconds, at the time I thought those moments would never end. There was absolutely nothing I could do—I wasn't even driving. I thought about that Sunday morning two days ago on Easter Sunday evening. We were running an errand and came to an intersection. The sun shone so brightly that I couldn't read the street sign and missed the turn. I flashed on the memory of the Sunday morning drive to church with Delmer.

If you're like me, you don't like feeling powerless. We like to be in control. We like to be in the driver's seat. We don't want to be blindsided by situations and circumstances we are powerless to control—like the current pandemic for example. There are things we can do, things we can manage: we can keep our distance, we can shelter in place, we can wash our hands and use hand sanitizer. We can wear facemasks and gloves when we go to the grocery store, the pharmacy or the post office. When I engage in these practices I feel like I'm making a difference and managing my risk. Who knows, maybe I'm saving lives. Then I watch the news, listen to the radio, or read the newspaper and I'm reminded of all the things I can't control. I come face to face with my powerlessness. Again.

Writing from a Roman jail, St. Paul shared some of his core convictions with the Christians in Philippi:

> Rejoice in the Lord always; again I will say, Rejoice. Let your gentleness be known to everyone. The Lord is near. Do not worry about anything but in everything by prayer and supplication with thanksgiving let your requests be made known to God. And the peace of God, which surpasses all understanding, will guard your hearts and your minds in Christ Jesus. (Phil 4:4–7)

Paul knew a thing or two about powerlessness. In his second letter to the church at Corinth, he wrote about his struggle with what he referred to as "a thorn in the flesh." He prayed and prayed and prayed for deliverance—to no avail. He was powerless to do anything to rid himself of the thorn. (No one knows what the thorn was; chances are if he wanted his readers to know, he would have informed them.) Here's where it gets interesting: Jesus answered his prayer but it wasn't the answer Paul was expecting: "My grace is sufficient for you, for power is made perfect in weakness" (2 Cor 12:9).

The Message translation of this passage is helpful: "My grace is enough; it's all you need. My strength comes into its own in your weakness." I have no doubt that St. Paul engaged in all the prayer practices he wrote about to the Philippians: Grateful to God, re-joicing in the Lord's nearness and free of worry, he offered up his prayer request trusting that God's peace would guard his heart and mind. He prayed those prayers over and over and over again. In the course of his prayers, he had a revelation: God's grace was all he needed. It was enough; it was sufficient; nothing else mattered. God's strength was manifest in his weakness. Miraculously, he learned to live with the thorn.

After relearning the sufficiency and wonder of God's grace, St. Paul went on to write to the Corinthians: "Therefore I am content with weaknesses, insults, hardships, persecutions, and calamities for the sake of Christ; for whenever I am weak, then I am strong" (2 Cor 12:10). Me, I could learn a lot from St. Paul's hard-won wisdom and humility. My defaults are self-reliance and self-sufficiency. I want to be in control. I don't like feeling, let alone *being* powerless. St. Paul was able to surrender to God's grace and providence. In his letter to the Philippians he wrote:

> I have learned to be content with whatever I have. I know what it is to have little, and I know what it is to have plenty. In any and all circumstances I have learned the secret of being well fed, and of going hungry, of having plenty and of being in need. I can do all things through Christ who strengthens me. (Phil 4:11–13).

Turns out, St. Paul wasn't so powerless after all. He could do anything that needed doing. St. Paul could endure being cooped up in a Roman jail writing pastoral letters even though he would have preferred to have been face to face with the churches he planted and the congregations he loved. He prayed to be relieved of the thorn in his flesh; he wasn't, and he learned to live with it. Elsewhere St. Paul wrote: "By the grace of God I am who I am" (1 Cor 15: 10). Graced, forgiven and free, St. Paul learned to be content whether he had everything he needed and then some, or was needy, hungry and had little. He could do all these things and more through Christ who strengthened him. God's grace was enough. Period.

The Assignment of Impossible Tasks

April 17, 2020

I can do all things through Christ who strengthens me.
(Phil 4:13)

I AM AN OBLATE AT St. Andrew's Abbey, a Benedictine monastery in Valyermo, California. An oblate is someone who desires to follow the Rule of St. Benedict, without committing to the communal life of monks.

One of my daily devotional practices is to read a portion of the Rule of St. Benedict from Sister Joan Chittister's book, *The Rule of Benedict: Insights for the Ages*, each day. Over the years Sr. Chittister and St. Benedict's wisdom and counsel have shaped my pastoral ministry and my personal faith, hope and love. One of my favorite readings in Benedict's rule is chapter 68, "Assignment of Impossible Tasks."

Benedict says that a monk may be assigned a burdensome task or something they cannot do. "If so," he writes:

> They should, with complete gentleness and obedience, accept the order given them . . . If the weight of the burden is too great, then they should discuss this with the prioress or abbot, the servant leader of the community. If after the explanation the abbot or prioress is still determined to hold to their original order, then the junior

must recognize that this is best. Trusting in God's help, they must in love, obey.[1]

Sr. Chittister's meditation on this chapter in the Rule of St. Benedict is instructive:

> The straight and simple truth is that there are some things in life that must be done, even when we don't want to do them, even when we believe we can't do them . . . The reality is that we are often incapable of assessing our own limits, our real talents, our true strength, our necessary ordeals. If parents, teachers, employers, and counselors somewhere hadn't insisted, we would have never gone to college or stayed at the party or tried the work or met the person or begun the project that, eventually changed our lives and made us more than we ever knew ourselves to be.[2]

I have found this passage from the Rule of St. Benedict, along with St. Paul's counsel that "I can do all things through Christ who strengthens me," to be especially helpful while living through the coronavirus pandemic. I want to remember and be mindful of the gospel truth that by God's grace I can do what needs to be done.

What needs doing isn't always extraordinary or herculean feats of derring-do; sometimes it's the tedious and repetitive duty of staying put and not venturing out. Sometimes it's being content with things as they are, rather than things being the way I would like them to be. I am learning, one day at a time, that the Triune God is at the ready to provide us with the grace, grit, strength, and stamina to do the things that need doing and to let go of the things that for now, I simply cannot do.

---

1. Chittister, *The Rule of St. Benedict: Insights for the Ages*, 173–174.
2. Chittister, *The Rule of St. Benedict: Insights for the Ages*, 173–174.

Looking For the Good

April 21, 2020

Finally, beloved, whatever is true, whatever is honorable,
whatever is just, whatever is pure, whatever is pleasing,
whatever is commendable, if there is any excellence and
if there is anything worthy of praise, think about these
things. (Phil 4:8)

IN THE SUMMER OF 2016, I traveled to Rwanda with a group of
eighteen high school teachers, college professors, one university
student and Carl Wilkens, the only American to remain in Kigali,
Rwanda, during the 1994 genocide against the Tutsi. As a board
member of World Outside My Shoes, the 501(c)3 non-profit that
supports Carl's work as a storyteller, speaker, workshop leader and
author, I was along for the ride. Literally.

It was our first full day in Kigali. As we settled into our seats
on the bus en route to visit the Kigali Genocide Memorial, the final
resting place of the remains of more than 250,000 victims of the
Rwandan genocide, Carl began to prepare us for the day ahead.
After a few introductory remarks, Carl instructed us—*invited* us—
to "look for the good." I had visited the Kigali Genocide Memorial
on previous visits to Rwanda and so I had some idea of what to

expect. What I wasn't expecting was to be invited to "look for the good." But I did, as did all the members of our group.

Carl's invitation to look for the good is a key to who he is and what his life is all about. I first learned about Carl and his work in Rwanda during the genocide while watching the 2004 PBS Frontline documentary, *The Ghosts of Rwanda*. Previously, I had done a fair amount of reading about the genocide, but I hadn't read about Carl. Sitting on the couch in our basement watching the television, I was stunned by the narrator's words after the first interview segment with Carl: "Carl Wilkens saved more lives during the 1994 genocide than the entire US government." The next day, I found an email address for Carl online. I wrote him and we met a few months later. We've been friends ever since.

After the first three weeks of the genocide, Carl started venturing out onto the streets of Kigali, working his way through roadblocks of angry, bloodstained soldiers and civilians armed with machetes and assault rifles in order to bring food, water and medicine to groups of orphans trapped around the city. Carl and his Rwandan co-workers helped save the lives of hundreds of people. His efforts are chronicled in his book, *I'm Not Leaving*, and the documentary film of the same name.

I was talking on the phone with Carl last week. His speaking engagements have been curtailed as a result of the coronavirus pandemic though he continues to Skype with students around the world and to do weekly Zoom "Finding the Good" sessions with educators in the U.S. During the course of our conversation, I wondered aloud, to Carl, "Can you imagine what it would have been like to go through a time like this"—our sheltering in place during the coronavirus pandemic— "twenty-five years ago without the technology we have available to us today?" Without missing a beat, Carl said, "Yes."

In an instant I remembered who I was talking to: Carl Wilkens, the man who had sheltered in place during the first three weeks of the Rwandan genocide without ever leaving his house. Truly, Carl had no problem whatsoever imagining being cooped up without technology as he quite literally sheltered in place. (Thankfully, Carl was in daily radio contact with his wife Teresa who was in Nairobi, Kenya, with their three children and his parents.) When I apologized for my thoughtless remark, Carl laughed. As usual, he was as gracious as could be.

One of the things I'm noticing, slowly but surely, is all the good people are doing, all the sacrificial acts of love that people are performing, and all the gracious gifts people are giving. I'm not just talking about the heroics of doctors, nurses, and first responders. I'm talking about ordinary folks like you and me. People reaching out to people who are feeling isolated and anxious. People who are engaging in intentional and thoughtful acts of kindness; people who are staying in touch and checking in. People who are sewing masks; grocery shopping for folks who can't get out and countless other acts of intentional thoughtfulness and kindness.

In spite of the all the pain, loss and suffering, people are doing amazing things, engaging in good and godly acts of love and care. I want to remember—I don't want to forget—Carl's invitation to look for the good. And I want to remember St. Paul's counsel of what to focus on: "Whatever is true, whatever is honorable, whatever is just, whatever is pure, whatever is pleasing, whatever is commendable, if there is any excellence and if there is anything worthy of praise, think about these things" (Phil 4:8).

The Coincidence of the Day

April 24, 2020

The fruit of the Spirit is love, joy, peace, patience, kindness, generosity, faithfulness, gentleness and self-control. (Gal 5:22–23)

YESTERDAY, I WAS SITTING AT the kitchen table reading a novel and eating lunch. As I read about a character talking about punching his time card, Dontay, our-son-in-law, was talking to Emily—his wife and our daughter—about *his* time card (he's currently on paternity leave). I exclaimed, "Coincidence of the Day! You were talking about a time card and I'm reading about a character talking about a time card. Coincidence of the Day!"

For years I've made a big deal about the Coincidence of the Day. Sometimes my announcement of the day's coincidence is met with playful rolling of the eyes; now and then it's met with genuine surprise. I don't wax philosophical about the random nature of the cosmos or try to plumb the depths of the mystery of life—I simply embrace and celebrate the Coincidence of the Day. Period. Over the years there have been some humdingers.

The first one happened on Good Friday in 1975. I had just preached a sermon at the noon worship service at Shepherd By The Sea Lutheran Church in Malibu, California, where I was serving my first pastorate. During the sermon I quoted a line from Bob Dylan's song, "It's Alright Ma (I'm Only Bleeding)." After that service, I left for Santa Monica to preach at a Good Friday, "Seven Last Words" worship service. En route, by the side of the road, I saw Bob Dylan talking to a vendor at a makeshift produce stand by the Gulf Oil gas station. Honest. A big time, Good Friday, Co-incidence of the Day.

One of my all-time favorite coincidences of the day took place after a Sunday morning worship service when I was serving as pastor of Our Savior Lutheran Church in Issaquah, Washington. Pastor Ryan Fletcher and I were preaching a nine-week summer series on "The Fruit of the Spirit," based on Galatians 5. We had found corresponding readings for each one of the Spirit fruit that Paul wrote about in this chapter—love, joy, peace, patience, kind-ness, generosity, faithfulness, gentleness, and self-control—and we were digging deep to harvest all the Spirit fruit of this wonderful passage we could find.

After worship and the coffee hour we locked up the church and I headed for home, stopping at the Front Street Market to pick up some groceries. I noticed the young checkout clerk had words tattooed on the inside of her left forearm. I took a closer look. I couldn't believe my eyes. An hour or so after preaching a sermon on the fruit of the Sprit, someone with Gal 5:22–23 (both verses!) tattooed on her forearm was ringing up my groceries. I said to her, "You're not going to believe this but I'm the pastor of the Lutheran church down the street and I just preached a sermon on the fruit of the Spirit." She looked at me in surprise and laughed.

For quite a few mornings now, after I make myself a cup of coffee and sit down to get my bearings for another day of shelter-ing in place. I read Gal 5:22–23. You'd think I'd have memorized it by now but it seems I often leave one out so I decided it was best to just look it up on my phone. I sit and read it and pray it hoping that by God's grace I will, in my interactions with others—in the house and virtually, via text, phone, email, and Zoom—live a spiri-tually fruitful day. Day in and day out, I'm finding it as daunting at times as it was when I was interacting with all kinds of people face to face, before we were ordered to stay put and stay safe. Like most folks I'm a work in progress. Like most folks, I'm grateful that God's grace is sufficient for the day. You too? Wonderful. Let's call that the Coincidence of the Day!

Living With Loss
April 28, 2020

When Jesus saw Mary weeping, and the Jews who came
with her also weeping, he was greatly disturbed in spirit
and deeply moved. He said, "Where have you laid Lazarus?"
They said, Lord, come and see. Jesus began to weep.
(John 11:33–35)

See, the home of God is among mortals. God will dwell
with them; they will be his peoples, and God himself
will be with them; God will wipe away every tear from
their eyes. Death will be no more; mourning and crying
and pain will be no more, for the first things have passed
away. (Rev 21:3–4)

I'VE NEVER SEEN ANYTHING LIKE it: The deceased's nephew took
his place on a pew in the front row of the church, as his uncle's
memorial service was about to begin. There was nothing especially
unusual about that. What was unusual was that the young man was
holding a bunched-up hand towel; not a handkerchief or a pack of
tissues; a hand towel. He was ready to shed some serious tears and
do some heavy-hearted grieving over the death of his uncle.

Living With Loss

We're living in a time of catastrophic loss. The numbers are numbing. According to CBS News and Johns Hopkins University, the number of coronavirus cases in the U.S. passed one million today as the death toll climbed to more than 57,000 nationwide. There have been over three million cases worldwide and more than 213,000 deaths globally.

What's more, due to sheltering in place and social distancing, people who are mourning the loss of loved ones from COVID-19 as well as other causes, natural and unnatural, are grieving in isolation. They are shedding tears in solitude. Funerals, memorial services and burials are being postponed and delayed. It's grief compounded by grief. My heart goes out to people living with loss, unable to receive the gift of the loving presence of family members and friends or the comfort and consolation of loved ones.

A couple of weeks ago I shared with some chaplain friends an Elizabeth Barber essay in the *New Yorker*, titled "The Plight of A Hospital Chaplain During the Coronavirus Pandemic: How Do You Comfort the Suffering When You're Not Allowed in the Room." One of those chaplains is Henrik Christopherson, who serves a hospital in Southern Illinois. He wrote me back and thanked me for the article. Then he shared his experiences working the "Easter Vigil" shift at the hospital.

> As chaplains we are called into COVID-19 rooms, doing our best to speak with them when they are not exhausted and/or sleeping. As you may suspect we call families as much as we are able and try to be a support to them. The biggest "surge" has been our time spent with nurses and staff who soldier on under so much uncertainty (and I talk to every housekeeping person I can find! They are the forgotten ones that are often terrified!) Many nurses live away from their own families, which is really tough on them. Yet our numbers in Central Illinois are small compared to New York City. We've had our sad deaths from COVID-19 too.
>
> I worked the "vigil" of Easter weekend. When I'm the only chaplain in the hospital, there is no telling what the range of "crisis interventions" I might get called into.

It started on Saturday with a twenty-something African American victim of a gunshot wound. We never did get his name. He died nameless. Then, I went to the bedside of a 25-year-old women suffering from a heroin overdose. (Her parents had to visit her one at a time since the hospital is on lockdown). The young woman's mother, who is Pentecostal, was in denial that her daughter (in a coma and on a ventilator) would die. The father, who was also Pentecostal, simply wanted justice for the people who sold her bad drugs in the bus terminal.

Early Sunday morning there was a death in the Newborn Intensive Care Unit (a child who was 56 days old.) Next, I was paged to the room of a 96-year-old Lutheran. She was very clear and attentive, just "longing" to go home! She wanted Easter texts read to her. As I read the Easter gospel from Matthew 28, where Jesus shows up unexpectedly to the women, I almost lost it. These texts speak into grief. For some reason, I cried as I sang "Christ the Lord is risen today!"

I said "Happy Easter" to staff that I passed in the hallway. I was haunted by the response of one of the nurses as it dawned on her, "Yeah, you're right, I almost forgot it was Easter!" I thought, "I had been on a roller-coaster of emotions overnight, and you 'forget' it is Easter?? How can you do that?" All bets are off if it's not Easter! [1]

I'm grateful for the reality check of Henrik's account of his Easter Vigil chaplaincy visits. Though I can't fathom the magnitude of the losses we're living with, Henrik's poignant and personal account brought me to the brink of tears. The Psalmist writes that God keeps count of our tears, another testimony to the God of love who knows us better than we know ourselves. (Ps 56:8) The agony of Jesus in the aftermath of the death of his friend Lazarus reminds me that Jesus knew and experienced the pain of loss and grief, confirming the witness of Hebrews:

> For we do not have a high priest who is unable to sympathize with our weaknesses, but we have one who in every respect has been tested as we are, yet without sin. Let us

1. Christopherson, *Personal Correspondence.*

therefore approach the throne of grace with boldness, so that we may receive mercy and find grace to find help in time of need (4:15–16).

Like you, I am sheltering in place and living with loss. We are alone and we are together as we pray and grieve, holding onto the hope that the God of love holds us in the palm of God's hand and promises new heaven and new earth where death will be no more, nor mourning and crying and pain, for the first things have passed away.

Lily Packed a Facemask

May 1, 2020

As God's chosen ones, holy and beloved, clothe
yourselves with compassion, kindness, humility,
meekness, and patience. Bear with one another and, if
anyone has a complaint against another, forgive each
other; just as the Lord has forgiven you, so you must
also forgive. Above all, clothes yourselves with love,
which binds everything together in perfect harmony.
(Col 3:1–15)

OUR BAGS WERE PACKED AND we were ready to go. After more than
six weeks of sheltering in place in Texas with our daughter Emily,
our son-in-law Dontay, four-year old Lily and her two week-old
sister Ashton, we were flying home. Our original plan was to be in
Texas for Ashton's birth, but we weren't planning on being there
for six weeks. Like so many other things, our plans were disrupted
by the pandemic. But now it was time to go home.

Lily had packed her backpack and placed it next to our luggage. I didn't know if Lily was *pretending* to travel to Seattle with
us, or *actually* planning on flying home with us. As Emily looked
through the contents of Lily's backpack, she began to weep softly.
I knew Emily hated to see us go; after six weeks together, it was

hard to say goodbye. Emily gently lifted various items out of Lily's backpack: clothes, socks, some games, a snack and a facemask.

A facemask.

Lily packed one of the facemasks our friend Sue made for us to protect us when we were out and about in the world. Lily packed a facemask in her backpack. And I was undone.

I was undone because I didn't want to say goodbye. I was undone because I didn't know what it was going to be like for Lily or for me to spend our days apart after 46 days of meals together, walks, coloring, reading, and play. I was undone because even though Lily knows next to nothing about the pandemic, she knew that if she was going to go home with us she would need a facemask. I was undone as the cumulative effects of the pandemic and its collateral damage rolled over me like a flash flood of grief and sadness.

Yesterday during our weekly Zoom Bible study, we read in Eph 6:1–24 about "the whole armor of God." Having warned his readers about the struggle against "rulers, authorities, and the cosmic powers of this present darkness," St. Paul admonished them to, "take up the whole armor of God." St. Paul's "armor" list includes the belt of truth, the breastplate of righteousness, shoes for proclaiming the gospel of peace, the shield of faith, the sword of the Spirit (the word of God) and the helmet of salvation.

One Bible study participant wondered if we should add kindness to the armor list. I thought of St. Paul's words to the Colossians about how to suit up for life in Christ:

> As God's chosen ones, holy and beloved, clothe yourselves with compassion, kindness, humility, meekness, and patience . . . Above all, clothes yourselves with love, which binds everything together in perfect harmony. (Col 3:12, 14)

Whether one prefers the image of armor or the image of a clotheshorse all fitted out in compassion, kindness, humility, meekness, patience, and love, the point is the same. Whether sheltering in place, or out and about, we are interacting with others, and we need to be ready for whatever or whoever comes our way.

A full wardrobe outfits us for any and all occasions, preparing us for living our days and loving others.

In her book, *Wearing God: Clothing, Laughter, Fire, and Other Overlooked Ways of Meeting God,* Lauren Winner writes:

> Alexander MacLaren was a nineteenth-century Baptist minister in Manchester, England. In his commentary on Romans, I read this, 'It takes a lifetime to fathom Jesus; it takes a lifetime to appropriate Jesus, it takes a lifetime to be clothed with Jesus. And the question comes to each of us, have we "put off the old man with his deeds?" Are we daily, as sure as we put on our clothes in the morning, putting on Christ the Lord? [1]

Dr. Winner writes:

> I take out a note card and copy down MacLaren's words (informing the reader that she will tape the card to her closet door.) I become professional or hip, depending on what I am wearing. I feel different when I am wearing different clothes. I act different. I let my Talbot's suits and my vintage shirts remake me in their image. I want to let Jesus do the same. [2]

Wednesday morning, Dontay and Lily drove Ann and me to the airport. We said our goodbyes, unloaded our luggage and put on the uniform/armor of the day: Facemasks and gloves. The few travelers, airport personnel, and flight crews in the terminal kept their distance. Our flight was at about 25 per cent capacity. The airlines had not sold any middle seats and Ann and I had all of row eighteen to ourselves. Passengers in front of and behind us were wearing facemasks but a couple of passengers one row up and across the aisle were not. I resolved not to judge them, though it wasn't easy. Between the facemasks, the distancing and the hand sanitizer, I felt I had all the armor I needed. What I knew I needed even more was to be clothed in compassion, kindness, patience and love.

1. Winner, *Wearing God*, 41.
2. Winner, *Wearing God*, 42.

Unstuck in Time

May 5, 2020

Do not ignore this one act, beloved, with the Lord one
day is like a thousand years, and a thousand years are
like one day. (2 Pet 3:8)

I WOKE UP THURSDAY MORNING feeling like Billy Pilgrim in Kurt
Vonnegut's novel, *Slaughterhouse Five*: "unstuck in time." We'd been
sheltering in place in the central time zone in Texas for over six
weeks. I was living in Texas, but working in Washington. Sunday
morning worship was at 10:00 am in Washington but at 12:00
noon in Texas. Weekly staff meetings, Tuesday prayer gatherings,
and Thursday Bible studies were also at 10:00 am in Washington
and noon in Texas. Most days, I'd look at the Texas clock and wonder where the day had gone. Living in one time zone and working
in another was disorienting.

After flying home last Wednesday, I woke up Thursday morning and looked at the clock. It showed 5:00 am. I thought to myself,
"okay, it's 5:00 am here; that means it's 7:00 am in Texas." I was trying to re-orient myself, time zone wise. Just to be sure, I checked
my cellphone. It said 6:00 am (which meant 8:00 am, Texas time.)
I was confused. Then I remembered: we were in Texas for the day-
light's savings time change; at our home in Issaquah, the clocks

hadn't been moved forward one hour like the Texas clocks had. I changed the time on a few of our clocks and settled in for the day. Then I realized that the Thursday Bible study was at 10:00 am Washington time and I was now living and working in Washington time. Whew!

No matter the day or the hour, I sometimes feel like I'm using mental and spiritual muscles that I have rarely if ever exercised; it's like I've gone from walking around the block one day to running a marathon the next day. (Now that I think about it, it's actually more a matter of going from running marathons to walking around the block, metaphorically speaking.) Social distancing and sheltering in place have deactivated our usually busy, *going here* and *rushing there* daily lives to a crawl. We are being pushed and pulled and stretched in new and sometimes exasperating ways. St. Peter's counsel that with the Lord one day is like a thousand years and a thousand years are like one day makes curious, mystical sense.

Mindful of the twelve-step wisdom of Alcoholics Anonymous to take one day at a time, I am striving, by God's grace, to make the most of each day. Social distancing and sheltering in place limit my options, but it doesn't obliterate them. Like you, I'm unable to do things I love doing: I can't meet a friend for coffee or go to a movie theater; I can't attend a concert or visit a bookstore; I'm unable to gather with people for worship.

The truth of the matter is that thanks to technology, I'm able to do a lot. FaceTime Sunday morning worship is a joyous grace; all sorts of musicians are offering online concerts; on Sunday evening Ann and I watched a movie courtesy of the Seattle International Film Festival's website; I can and have ordered books online; and a friend and I are going to do Zoom coffee sometime soon.

In his book, *Time and the Art of Living*, Robert Grudin, invites his readers to make the most of the day:

> You have a day to spare and wish to use it well. You see yourself in a kind of compartment of time whose immediate walls are last night's and tonight's sleep. Look beyond these walls and back at the present from imaginary mirrors placed in the past and the future. Think of the

choices and events that brought you where you are; think of what you once wished or expected to have achieved by this point. Imagine what you will think of this period some time in the future. Will you think or do anything today that is worthy of future memory? Try to make the present memorable; or, failing this, review daily what is important about the present period in your life. In so doing you will enrich time. [1]

Smack dab in the middle of the Book of Lamentations—a bracing and painful testimony to the suffering of Israel in the aftermath of the destruction of Jerusalem and Israel's exile to Babylon—the poet writes these amazing words: "The steadfast love of the Lord never ceases, his mercies never come to an end; they are new every morning; great is your faithfulness. 'The Lord is my portion,' says my soul, 'therefore I will hope in him'"(Lam 3:22–24).

No matter the day or the hour, the God of all grace, forever faithful, is our hope. I want to remember the promise of God's steadfast love and endless daily mercies in the dizzying dance of my days.

1. Grudin, *Time and the Art of Living*, 30–31.

Risk Management

May 8, 2020

A lawyer asked Jesus a question, to test him, "Teacher, which commandment in the law is greatest?" Jesus said to him, "You shall love the Lord your God with all your heart, and with all your soul, and with all your mind. This is the greatest and first commandment. And a second is like it: 'You shall love your neighbor as yourself.' On these two commandments hang all the law and the prophets." (Matt 22:36–40)

It was a Sunday morning in the summer of 2014. We had just commissioned our Peru Mission Team. A group of high school students and adults, including me, would depart for Lima, Peru, the following day. As I greeted the departing worshippers at the door of the sanctuary, one of the parents, a law enforcement retiree, shook my hand and said to me, "Make sure you bring my baby home safe." His son was a high school senior. I took his father's request to heart. Big time.

As our group met up at Seattle-Tacoma International Airport the next day, I could feel the pressure of my responsibilities mounting. I was the pastor. I was more or less in charge. Once we arrived in Lima, we would reunite with Henrik and Patty Christopherson, members of our congregation who had served as missionaries in Peru for over twenty-five years. They would be our guides and our shepherds. Still and all, I was the pastor and if anything went wrong, I would have to answer for it. I carried that group, literally. We had a packet with everyone's medical releases and contact information. I never let those papers out of my sight.

After a few days in Peru, it slowly dawned on me: we were on a mission trip and there were both avoidable risks and unavoidable ones. There were things we could control, and things we couldn't. We got lost en route to the city of Cuzco where we planned to spend the night and catch a train for Machu Picchu the next day. There was a detour, and then another detour, and then another. After three detours, our driver realized we were lost. Unavoidable risk. Thankfully we found our way to Cuzco. On another day, several students wanted to go on a hike; I had my reservations; I thought it was an avoidable risk. The other adults wisely overruled me. I'd let my anxiety get the better of me. Someone slipped on the hike but the injury was minor. All the hikers returned safe and sound.

It was a huge relief, and a big burden lifted, when we returned home and I said my final goodbyes at SeaTac's baggage claim area. The mission trip was life changing for all of the participants. We had more than our share of wonderful adventures and memories a plenty. We managed our risks and had minimal mishaps.

I've been thinking a lot about risk management. After spending four hours in an airplane on a flight from Dallas to Seattle last week, I decided to stay put for a couple weeks. (I wanted to manage avoidable risks.) Other than going for walks, I haven't left the house for a week, except for one quick trip to get groceries. I drove to the store, parked my car, and put on my facemask. While shopping, I was surprised by the number of people who were not keeping six feet apart or wearing facemasks. Doing my best to manage my judgmental thoughts (Jesus discouraged this sort of thing) I got my groceries and made a beeline for the car.

What I keep re-learning is that I am hardwired to think about me and mine, not you and yours. It's my default. Call it human sin or human nature; call it whatever you want—I'm broken and more often than not, I put me first and others second. I don't want to get COVID-19 and so I keep my distance and I wear my mask and I use hand sanitizer to avoid risking contact with others for my own sake.

When others don't wear facemasks or keep their distance, I'm tempted to get all riled up. And then it dawns on me; the mini-epiphany, the realization that I am and we are in the process of undergoing a great big life-changing paradigm shift: At my mindful neighbor loving best, I'm doing what I'm doing for your sake *and* mine. (The Center for Disease Control and Prevention encourages people to wear face coverings in public; not just to protect ourselves but also those around us.) So, if you keep your distance and wear a facemask then you're a neighbor lover. You're doing what you're doing for your sake and for our sakes. And when we do, we'll flatten the curve and manage the risks and get through this together.

Jesus and the Center for Disease Control have at least one thing in common: they both want all of us to take care of ourselves, and each other. Believe it or not, the commandment to love our neighbors as ourselves didn't originate with Jesus. It's from Leviticus 19:18, which says, "you shall not take vengeance or bear a grudge against any of your people, but you shall love your neighbor as yourself." What's unique, what's extraordinary, is Jesus' teaching that by loving God with all we are, and loving our neighbors as ourselves, we are in fact living out the teachings of the law and the words of the prophets.

When we wear facemasks, we love our neighbors, as ourselves. When we practice social distancing, we love our neighbors as ourselves. When we shelter in place, we love our neighbor, as ourselves. Normally, typically, usually, neighbor loving is doing what's good for and/or on behalf of our neighbor. This current pandemic expression of neighbor love is counter-intuitive, and counter-cultural. For the living of these days, neighbor love as social distancing, face masking and staying put seems passive, even isolating. But it isn't. For the time being, it's simply lifesaving—for you, for me and for our neighbors.

Decisions

May 12, 2020

Whatever you do, in word or deed, do everything in the name of the Lord Jesus, giving thanks to God the Father through him. (Col 3:17)

A decision joins us to the eternal. It brings what is eternal into time. A decision raises us with a shock from the slumber of monotony. A decision breaks the magic spell of custom. A decision breaks the long row of weary thoughts. A decision pronounces its blessing upon even the weakest beginning, as long as it is a real beginning. Decision is the awakening to the eternal. (*Provocations: Spiritual Writings of Kierkegaard*, Soren Kierkegaard) [1]

"DECISION IS THE AWAKENING TO the eternal?" Really? Yes. I think Kierkegaard is spot on. Every day, each and every one of us is faced with decisions—big decisions; little decisions and no brainers. According to Dr. Joel Hoomans, of Roberts Wesleyan University, various online sources estimate "that an adult makes about 35,000

1. Kierkegaard, *Provocations: Spiritual Writings of Kierkegaard*, 3.

remotely conscious decisions each day." That number may sound astonishing, but according to researchers at Cornell University, we make 226.7 decisions each day on just food alone!

Decisions. We get up in the morning and the choices and decisions commence. Sure, many things are routine and habitual, but there are still countless choices and decisions to make. Dr. Hoomans offers a modest sampling of the choices we are faced with: What to eat? What to wear? What to do? What not to do? What to purchase?

Decisions. We choose what to believe and decide how we will vote. We decide who we will spend our time with. And, my favorite, we figure out "What do we say and how do we say it?" And that's not the half of it. Each one of our choices carries consequences both good and bad. "The ability to choose is an incredible and exciting power that we have each been entrusted with by our Creator and for which we have an obligation to be good stewards of," writes Dr. Hoomans.[2] Lots of our decisions are individual/personal and impact others; other decisions are corporate and impact individuals. Decisions.

Sammamish Hills Lutheran Church is in the process of making important decisions regarding life together that will be made corporately and have impacts for the congregation and its members. At tonight's church council meeting, council members will begin a conversation about working through the process of aligning the mission, ministries, and programs of SHLC with Gov. Jay Inslee's four phases of re-opening, being mindful of and prioritizing the safety and well-being of church members, friends and neighbors. Decisions.

Over the years, when facing difficult decisions, I have often turned to the counsel of Fr. Gale Webbe and his essay, "Decisions." Fr. Webbe's essay on decisions is from his book, *The Night and Nothing*. Here's some of his wisdom on decision-making:

> Human intelligence develops its highest powers and uses them rightly when strengthened by love and when protected by prayer. In this calm, protracted colloquy we are

2. Hoomans, 35,000 *Decisions: The Great Choices of Strategic Leaders.*

not simply talking with other humans, wise or unwise, but with Wisdom and Truth himself. Furthermore, in such an exercise, God is talking with us—a fact which removes this practice from any reasonable charge of magic. There is ample sober testimony that this approach brings about correct choices. The most subtle decisions, affecting whole lives and generations, can and do resolve into certainties when we give God time enough to make his loving will clear to our hard heads and hearts.

A more important result of this practice is the clarification of motive. The end of time available to us—a week, it may be—before we must decide can leave us in a condition like this: "I do not know, even yet. God has not shown me which course to take, or in my deafness, I have not heard him. It may be that both courses are good and that one is merely higher. I do know now, however, that if I choose course X the motives will be entirely sound at my present level of development. Therefore I can take that course without a bit of fear or worry." This is a sound conclusion because God uses motives, like love, to far better advantage than he uses wisdom. A decision based on honest motives works out so surely for good that it is entirely true to say that even if it is the wrong decision, it will be the right one. [3]

The day is new and so far, my decisions have been shaped by my morning practices, routines, habit and schedule. I've already made a few decisions and there are more to come. I'm counting on and trusting God will have enough time to make his loving will clear.

3. Webbe, *The Night and Nothing*, 67–68.

Patience

May 15, 2020

Love is patient. (1 Cor 13:4)

I CONFESS THESE TIMES ARE trying my patience. Sheltering in place, I wonder how long staying home to stay safe will go on. Isolating, I think to myself, *Where's the finish line?* On the rare occasion when I'm out and about, I realize that my patience is wearing thin. Quick to judge, my patience is in short supply as I look at my shopping neighbors and silently say to myself: *Why aren't you keeping your distance? I am! Why aren't you wearing a mask? I am!*

According to *Webster's New World Dictionary,* "patience is the state, quality, ability or fact of being patient, which is the will or ability to wait or endure without complaint. Patience is bearing or enduring pain, trouble, and difficulties without complaining, or losing self-control or making a disturbance. Patience is calmly tolerating delay, confusion and inefficiency." Ouch!

My cellphone NRSV Bible's subheading for 1 Corinthians 13 is, "The Gift of Love." After writing about things like eloquence, prophetic powers, understanding mysteries, having knowledge, mountain moving faith, sacrificial giving and their utter uselessness without love, St. Paul writes about what love *is,* and, *isn't.* The first thing he says love *is,* is patient.

Various translations of "love is patient" are instructive for understanding what "love is patient" means: "Love never gives up" (The Message). "Love waits patiently" (Raymond F. Collins). "Love's great-hearted" (N.T. Wright). "Charity suffereth long" (King James Version); and yes, "Love is patient" (English Standard Version, New International Version, and the New Revised Standard Version).

In St. Paul's letter to the Galatians, he includes patience as a fruit of the spirit. People who are patient can wait it out. I think of patience as the ability go the distance with a person or that situation. When I think of patience, I think of Monica, the mother of St. Augustine, who before he was a bishop, theologian or saint, was an unbeliever who tested his mother's patience so much that she prayed for years that he would come to his senses and come to faith. No wonder, St. Monica is the patron saint of patience.

In his book, *Love Within Limits*, (a book about 1 Corinthians 13) Lewis Smedes, writes of love as patience, using the synonym, "longsuffering." He writes:

> When we talk about the power to be longsuffering, we are talking plainly about real suffering for a long time. We are talking about digging in daily, renewing over and over again to accept what we do not want and cannot change, making no bones about not wanting it, and yet determining to live with it and rejoice *in* it . . . Longsuffering is not passive. It is a tough, active, aggressive style of life. It takes power of soul to be longsuffering. [1]

I don't know about you, but right about now, I could do with a daily dose of the patience that is love. If all things are possible, then patience is a daily, moment-by-moment possibility. Mindful of God's love for me, I can learn to practice patience with others; I can cut them some slack and give them a break. If God is love and love is patient, then God's love can strengthen me for patiently loving others.

1. Smedes, *Love Within Limits*, 2–3.

Burdens

May 19, 2020

Come to me, all you that are weary and are carrying heavy burdens, and I will give you rest. Take my yoke upon you, and learn from me; for I am gentle and humble in heart, and you will find rest for your souls. For my yoke is easy, and my burden is light. (Matt 11:28–30)

PRETTY MUCH EVERYONE IS FEELING the overwhelming burdens of life and work during the coronavirus pandemic. Parents, who are working from home and dealing with the stress of work/life balance, are also dealing with the added burden of helping their children with online classes. Adult children are coping with the burdens of aging parents who need their support and assistance. Family members, neighbors and friends are living with the burdens of job loss, loss of income, and anxiety.

All of us are living with disruptions that require us to adjust, adapt and cope with countless changes and their unanticipated consequences. There are no quick fixes to the current state of affairs and little, if any, collective experiential wisdom to draw on. It often feels like we're making it up as we go along. We're doing our best, but it's not easy. Sometimes the added burdens (whatever or whoever they are) feel like more than we can bear.

I'm exploring a threefold approach to burden bearing that I believe applies anytime, but especially during times like these. Three biblical passages inform my thinking on this: Isa 46:1–4, Matt 11:28–30, and Gal 6:2. Isaiah compares the burden of Babylon's idols, on the animals that carry them, with the God of Jacob, who carries us:

"Listen to me, O house of Jacob, all the remnant of the house of Israel, who have been borne by me from your birth, carried from the womb; even to your old age I am he, even when you turn gray I will carry you. I have made, and I will bear; I will carry and I will save 46:3–4).

Jesus offers soul rest to all who are weary and carrying heavy burdens. I love Frederick Dale Bruner's translation of Matt 11:28–30 in *Matthew: A Commentary*:

"Come here to me, all of you who are struggling and carrying too much, and I will refresh you! Here, take my yoke upon you, and learn from me, because I am gentle and simple at heart, and you will experience refreshing deep down in your souls. You see, my yoke is easy to wear and my burden is light to carry."[1]

Dr. Bruner writes: "Jesus invites those who are having a hard time of it, those for whom life is hard work and those who feel overwhelmed." Thank God for Jesus' all-comers invitation list. No one's left out. Every one of us has a 24/7 all-access pass to the source of Spirit, soul refreshment, and renewal. Dr. Bruner acknowledges that our life is a succession of unavoidable burdens and responsibilities. "Jesus realizes that the most restful gift he can give the tired is a new way to carry life, a fresh way to bear responsibilities," he writes.[2]

St. Paul invites the Christians in Galatia to bear one another's burdens and fulfill the law of Christ. Our life together, worship, fellowship, and our prayers, encourage, strengthen and sustain us. I'm learning to remember that God is bearing us up and Jesus is the source of refreshment and renewal. Mindful of these truths, I

---

1. Bruner, *Matthew, A Commentary, Volume 1*, 537.
2. Bruner, *Matthew, A Commentary, Volume 1*, 538.

am grateful that bearing each other's burdens, we can lighten up and carry on one day at a time.

Faith

May 22, 2020

The apostles said to the Lord, "Increase our faith!" The Lord replied, "If you had faith the size of a mustard seed, you could say to this mulberry tree, 'Be uprooted and planted in the sea,' and it would obey you." (Luke 17:5–6)

WE'RE A CHURCH, SO WE use the word *faith* a lot. We say we are a *faith community*; we say we care about *faith formation*; we confess our *faith* in the words of the Apostles' Creed. We often use the words *faith, trust,* and *belief* interchangeably, suggesting that they are one and the same thing. I believe they are, more or less. As a child, I was taught that faith was simple: faith, is believing in Jesus, trusting that God loves me and is always with me.

My faith is fortified by the Holy Scriptures, my life experiences and by the loving and supportive relationships of others. Now and then I have my doubts, but mostly I'm a believer.

Lately, I've been thinking a lot about faith. I want to get a fix on what faith is and what faith does. I want to define and clarify what I mean when I use the words *faith, trust* and *belief*—and I want to do so with as much precision as possible. The problem with my little project is that faith is a lot of things. The dictionary says that faith is a noun, then it says faith is a verb. Faith *the noun* is defined as belief and trust in God; a belief in the traditional doctrines of a religion. Faith *the verb* is defined as "faithing." I'm pretty sure that trusting is a better way to express faith the verb, so let's go with that.

I scanned the books on my bookshelves, examining their table of contents and indices for compelling and incisive words of wisdom about faith. Some authors go on and on. Others get to the point with admirable brevity. *Crazy Talk: A Not-So-Stuffy Dictionary of Theological Terms,* edited by Rolf A. Jacobson, is helpful here.

> Part trust, part knowledge, part following—faith can't be reduced to a few steps; it is a way of life, the walk of a lifetime, one day at a time . . . Faith is a hard concept to understand. Don't believe us; just read the Bible.

Quoting Luke 17:5–6 (see above) *Crazy Talk* continues:

> Jesus wasn't exactly serious—he was just funnin' with them a little so that they would understand something about faith, because the point isn't how much faith you have; the point is whom your faith is in. [1]

This definition implies that faith is more than a matter of belief or trust; faith is relationship too. In his *Small Catechism,* Martin Luther says that faith is a gift. In his explanation to the Third Article of the Apostles' Creed, "I believe in the Holy Spirit, the holy catholic church, the communion of saints, the forgiveness of sins, the resurrection of the body, and the life everlasting," Luther writes:

> I believe that by my own understanding or strength I cannot believe in Jesus Christ my Lord or come to him. But instead the Holy Spirit has called me through the gospel, enlightened me with his gifts, made me holy, and kept me in the true faith, just as he calls, gathers, enlightens and makes holy the whole Christian church on earth

---

1. Jacobson, *Crazy Talk,* 66.

and keeps it with Jesus Christ in the one common, true faith. [2]

The Triune God as confessed in the creeds—Father, Son, and Holy Spirit—is the one in whom we place our trust. Sometimes I experience faith and hope as two sides of the same coin. My faith in God's loving presence is strengthened by my experiences of God's faithfulness. At the same time, the promise of God's faithfulness gives me hope. Early in the pandemic, I started working on a playlist, or a mix tape, of songs I thought would be a good soundtrack for the living of these days. These songs keep me anchored in faith and hope.

Hiss Golden Messenger's "When the Wall Comes Down" is a winsome litany of faith and hope, a big picture view of a future time of release and deliverance. Jakob Dylan's "Nothing But the Whole Wide World" cheers my spirit. It reminds me of God's love for us, and the assurance that I can—we can—endure, doing what needs to be done (or doing nothing at all). "He Will See You Through" by Rhiannon Giddens soothes my soul and calms my fears, helping me remember God's faithfulness.

I love the following quote from St. Francis de Sales. It's the kind of counsel that helps me trust in God's faithfulness, no matter what. It's a beautiful example of faith the verb:

> I recommend to you holy simplicity. Look straight in front of you and not at those dangers you see in the distance. As you say, to you they look like armies, but they are only willow branches; and while you are looking at them you may take a false step. Let us be firmly resolved to serve God with our whole heart and life. Beyond that, let us have no care about tomorrow. Let us think only of living today well, and when tomorrow comes, it also will be today and we can think about it then. [3]

---

2. Luther, *Luther's Small Catechism*, 16.

3. de Sales and de Chantal, *Letters of Spiritual Direction*, 98–99.

America's Other Pandemic

May 29, 2020

God has told you, O mortal, what is good; and what does
the Lord require of you but to do justice, and to love
kindness and to walk humbly with your God? (Mic 6:8)

IT WAS SEPTEMBER 1992. I was in Atlanta, Georgia, for a meeting of facilitators trained by the Foundation for Community Encouragement (FCE) a now defunct non-profit educational organization founded by M. Scott Peck, the author of, *The Road Less Traveled*. After a couple days of meetings, we had a free afternoon. Several of us wanted to visit the Martin Luther King Jr. Center for Nonviolent Social Change and Ebenezer Baptist Church in Atlanta. So after lunch, we headed out.

We took a Metropolitan Atlanta Rapid Transit Authority train and then we boarded a city bus. Walking the last few blocks through a low-income, African-American neighborhood, I felt anxious. I asked my friend Delmer Chilton if it was safe. He turned and looked at me in astonishment. "Let me get this straight," Delmer said to me incredulously. "You want to visit the Dr. King Center and the Ebenezer Baptist Church but you don't want to walk through a Black neighborhood to get there?"

I don't like telling this story. Not one bit. I don't like fessing up to my broken, sin-sick fear of the other. But there you have it. A couple of years later, I was in Chicago, Illinois, for another meeting of FCE facilitators. I was in a conversation with one of our colleagues, an African-American professor at the University of Tennessee. He was a runner, but he told us that there was no way he would go for a run in the neighborhood surrounding the suburban retreat center where we were meeting. As a former runner myself, I didn't see the problem. Call it my naiveté; call it ignorance; call it cluelessness; call it racism. I didn't know what I was talking about, but he did.

As our nation mourns and marks the incomprehensible loss of one hundred thousand of our fellow citizens to the coronavirus pandemic, Americans are also grieving the murders of Ahmaud Arbery and George Floyd, the latest casualties in America's other, ongoing pandemic: racism. Jim Wallis calls racism, "America's original sin." There is no way to calculate the number of victims of this centuries-old pandemic. Is it hundreds of thousands? Millions? Out of curiosity, I Googled "How many people have died due to racism?" I couldn't find any numbers.

I listen to and watch the news. I read the newspaper. I try to stay informed. Sometimes I don't know what to think or feel. Sometimes I'm sad; sometimes I'm angry; sometimes I'm numb. A lot of the time, I feel powerless and don't know what to do. I write those words and remember a cartoon my friend Dan Pagoda drew for the *Wittenburg Do*or, a Christian satirical magazine. The one-panel drawing showed a crowd of people all wondering, "What can woman do? What can one man do?" Great questions. What *can* one person do? Who knows? What can you and I do together? What can you and I together with all the people of God do? Can we change the world?

I notice that my emotions are spiking of late. Maybe it's sheltering in place. Maybe it's fear of the coronavirus. Maybe it's the cumulative effects of living with less and less certainty about the future. Maybe it's the stress of all the changes we're going through and living with. (In a meeting of local ELCA pastors, Bishop

Shelley Bryan Wee told us that during a recent Conference of Bishops meeting, a presenter informed the bishops that "we've gone through twenty years of changes in two months!") Whatever it is, my emotions and feelings are *more*. My joy is greater; my fear is stronger; my fuse is shorter; my sadness and grief over all kinds of losses, is deeper.

As a nation, we are going through the wringer. The pandemic's countless impacts on the common good, education, the economy, job losses, institutions, communities of faith and on neighborhoods, workplaces, businesses, households and on us; it sometimes feel like it's just too much. I'm grateful for every single moment of stability, grace, and peace in the midst of bad news on too many fronts. Of all the daily battles I engage, more often than not fear, anxiety, and worry are at the top of the list. In Matt 6:27, Jesus asked if our worrying "would add a single hour to your span of life?" Then, in verse 34 he said, "Don't worry about tomorrow, for tomorrow will bring worries of its own. Today's trouble is enough for today. I need to take Jesus' words to heart. Everyday.

Writing to the Philippians, St. Paul said:

> Don't fret or worry. Instead of worrying, pray. Let petitions and praises shape your worries into prayers, letting God know your concerns. Before you know it, a sense of God's wholeness, everything coming together for good, will come and settle you down. It's wonderful what happens when Christ displaces worry at the center of your life. (4:6–7 MSG)

Here's my prayer: That the grace of God and the tender mercies of Jesus will flood my heart and mind and set me free to do justice, love kindness and walk humbly with God. I don't want to live in fear, especially fear of the other. I want to be a good neighbor and welcome the stranger. I want to be set free from my biases and prejudices. I can prevent the spread of the coronavirus by sheltering in place, washing my hands, social distancing and wearing a mask. I can prevent the spread of racism, by fighting my fears of the unknown other and following Jesus' great commandment to love my neighbor as myself. You can too. Together, we can do this.

Protestants

June 4, 2020

Seek the welfare of the city where I have sent you into
exile, and pray to the Lord on its behalf, for in its welfare
you will find your welfare. (Jer 29:7)

IT WAS A SATURDAY MORNING workday at the church. Danny and
I were weeding a small plot of land between the south side of the
sanctuary and the driveway. He was a retired member of the Los
Angeles Police Department and I was his pastor. We were talking
about the campus unrest of the 1960s and 1970s. To our mutual
amazement we discovered that we were both on campus on the
same day at California State University, Northridge (then known
as San Fernando Valley State College), when a peaceful protest
turned violent. He was inside the building and I was outside.

At the moment when the protest turned violent (a student
activist threw a concrete cigarette receptacle through a glass door)
members of the LAPD in riot gear poured out of all the doors on
the south side of the administration building. As the police fanned
out in every direction, students and protesters did too. Face to face
with Danny some twenty years later, I asked him how he felt that
day. "Scared," he said. "Me too," I replied. I don't remember who
spoke next or what was said. What I do remember was that though

we had been on opposite sides during a time of civil unrest, it did not estrange us in the here and now.

It's a beautiful Wednesday in downtown Issaquah. As I write, I'm sitting in my favorite spot and drinking in the view out the living room window. But I'm in a bubble; an oasis. Sheltering in place, I can't go out tonight even if I wanted to, due a curfew imposed by the mayor of Issaquah. It's my understanding that there will be a peaceful protest at Sammamish City Hall on Thursday afternoon. I can escape into the safety of my living room, but I can't escape the gnawing sense that the impacts of the social unrest following the murder of George Floyd are getting closer and closer to home.

I'm heartened by the "Message from Sammamish Police Department Chief Dan Pingrey," posted on the City of Sammamish website two days ago. Chief Pingrey writes:

> I've been monitoring the situation in Seattle and across the county and have been in constant contact with Sammamish Police Department staff, our City Manager, and Councilmembers. What happened to Mr. Floyd in Minneapolis is unconscionable, and I do not have words to adequately describe my outrage and frustration at the actions of the officer and the inaction of those officers who stood by and failed to intervene. My thoughts and prayers go out to the family and friends of Mr. Floyd . . .
>
> The Sammamish Police understand the frustration felt by so many and respect individuals' rights to protest and exercise their free speech. We will support our community in that effort if they choose to do so and keep all of you safe during that endeavor. The violence and destructive behavior that has recently taken place throughout our region is a travesty. It only takes away from the message that peaceful protesters are trying to make and does not allow our community and our society to move forward and heal. Each of us needs to look at what we do, what we say, and how we act and treat each other. Racism has no place in our society and breeds nothing but hate and discontent. It will not be tolerated in the City of Sammamish, regardless of the reason. [1]

1. Chief Dan Pingrey, *City of Sammamish, Washington Website*, June 2, 2020.

Lutherans know a thing or two about protests. Our DNA as Lutherans was forged in the Protestant Reformation of 1500s. For hundreds of years, Lutheran Christians have taken to the streets in response to the abuse of religious and civil authority and on behalf of peace and justice. In his essay "Before the Fall" (*The Wilson Quarterly*, Fall 2009), Andrew Curry chronicled the role of the church in the fall of the Berlin Wall and the reunification of East and West Germany in 1989 and 1990. According to Mr. Curry, the Protestant churches were officially "tolerated" by the German Democratic Republic (commonly known as East Germany), but they were under constant scrutiny. In the early 1980s, two pastors in Leipzig, East Germany's second largest city began holding regular Monday evening prayers for peace at St. Nicholas Church.

Attending church, let alone prayer meetings, could mean the end of careers or blackballing by universities. Curry writes:

> Under pressure from the authorities, attendance at the Monday peace prayers shrank to fewer than ten regulars by the mid-1980s. Slowly word got around and the Monday meetings started to grow. By February 1988, attendance had grown to 600. Mikhail Gorbachev's reforms, together with warming relations with the West, gave hope and energy to people all over the Soviet bloc.

Mr. Curry continues:

> The last straw came on May 7, 1989, when regular elections for local party officials across East Germany were exposed as fraudulent by a loose network of volunteers who observed the vote count at local precincts—a right enshrined in the East German constitution but never exercised in an organized way—and then gathered in churches to compare results . . . .After a summer break (some things in Germany are sacred, no matter the political situation) thousands of people showed up at the St. Nicolas Church on Monday, September 4. Monday demonstrations were held at Lutheran churches all over East Germany. A movement eight years in the making was growing exponentially.

On Monday, October 9, nearly 8,000 people crammed into St. Nicolas. Three other downtown churches opened their doors to accommodate the overflow. In the end, nearly 70,000 Leipzigers, a sixth of the city, poured into the streets in peaceful protest chanting "Keine Gewalt" ("No Violence") and what would become the iconic slogan of the opposition movement, "Wir sind das Volk" (We are the people.) The crowd carried their candles onto the ring road around the city center, marching past the Stasi (GDR Secret Service) headquarters and the hundreds of police gathered in front of the train station. "It was a great sign of hope. To hold a candle, you need both hands—one to hold the candle, and the other to keep it from being blown out," Pr. Christian Fuhrer said. "You can't hold a rock in your other hand."

The entire city was swept up. The sheer number of the people who peacefully took to Leipzig's streets disarmed the East German regime . . . "The decisive day was in Leipzig," Pr. Rainer Eppelman said. "They were ready to crack down on 30,000, but 30,000 didn't show up, 70,000 did. Seventy thousand people, who didn't know if they'd come home intact or see their families again. It was a heroic and enormous act of moral courage." The dam had broken. On October 16, a procession of 150,000 people marched around Leipzig's ring road; the week after it was 300,000, the crowds of Leipzigers joined by people from all over East Germany. On November 4, more than 500,000 people flooded Alexanderplatz in East Berlin . . . After the drama of the Monday demonstrations, the fall of the (Berlin) wall (November 9, 1989) was an anticlimax . . . Within a year, the two Germanys—divided for almost half a century—were reunited again and communism was a relic. [2]

I want to leave you with prayer for the neighborhood from, *Evangelical Lutheran Worship*:

> God our creator, by your holy prophet Jeremiah you taught your ancient people to seek the welfare of the cities in which they lived. We commend our neighborhood

2. Curry, *Before the Fall*, 16–35.

to your care, that it might be kept free from social strife and decay. Give us strength of purpose and concern for others, that we may create here a community of justice and peace where your will may be done; through your Son, Jesus Christ our Lord. Amen. [3]

---

3. *Evangelical Lutheran Worship,* 78.

Reality Checks

June 9, 2020

So we do not lose heart. Even though our outer nature is wasting away, our inner nature is being renewed day by day. (2 Cor 4:16)

I DON'T KNOW ABOUT YOU, but I don't like reality checks. I know they're useful, helpful, even life-saving, but I don't like them, not one bit. Reality checks interrupt my day and disrupt my life. I prefer to think that anything and everything is okay. I not only want to be able to shelter in place, I also want to stay in-doors and keep the world at bay. The older I get, the more I hope for uneventful days. I want to sail the little boat of my life through calm, peaceful waters. I don't like being caught off guard or unprepared for the storms of life coming up out of nowhere. I don't like contending with the unforeseen and the unanticipated facts of life. I don't like reality checks, but they keep coming, day in and day out.

Don't get me wrong; reality checks are not all bad. Reality checks can be good. Today is Saturday, an uneventful day. I take a phone call from my friend Craig Jorgensen, sharing the news that Buzz Kahn, one of our dearest friends, has died. I grieve for his family and I'm grateful for his life. The reality check is twofold. First, Buzz died; one day I too will die too. Second, my life wouldn't be the same if I hadn't met Buzz. He was the youth director at my home church in Los Angeles. In 1967, Buzz left California for a new job in Washington. Two years later, he hired me to work as a summer camp counselor during the summer of 1969. I met my wife Ann that summer. We've been married for almost fifty years. If Buzz hadn't left our church in Los Angeles to become the director of Lutheran Camping in Western Washington, I would have never met Ann. One day: two reality checks.

The reality checks are relentless. It feels like they have accelerated over the course of the last two weeks in the aftermath of the murder of George Floyd. As I have read about and listened to the experiences of people of color—especially African Americans—as well as public servants and members of law enforcement, I find the tsunami of reality checks at times overwhelming. Sometimes, I have to turn off the radio and the television, close up the laptop and fold the newspaper. Some days it's just too much.

Reality checks. In every congregation I have served, except for one, I have ministered to members of law enforcement, both local and federal. I have been a pastor to two police chiefs—one small town, one big city. I have experienced these persons as honorable, professional and compassionate members of the community. And every African American man I have ever known has had the experience of being pulled over by a police officer for "driving while Black." I struggle to find a way to hold these two realities in tension. I grieve for the experience of African American family members and friends who have been subjected to unjust and systemic racism. And I'm grateful to members of law enforcement I have known and served who day by day put their lives on the line to protect and serve us.

Writing to his friends at First Church, Corinth, St. Paul drilled down on the reality of life in Christ: "So we do not lose heart. Even though our outer nature is wasting away, our inner nature is being renewed day by day" (2 Cor 4:16). St. Paul's insight into the realities of life lived out day by day in Christ and in the world affirms the hard truth that our lives are subject to decay and death. True enough. But that's not all—not by a long shot. The good news is day by day God is renewing our faith, hope and love. Hence, we do not lose heart. No matter the joys, or the sorrows. That's a reality check I can live with.

It Always Seemed Longer
to the Finish Line Than I Thought

June 15, 2021

> Let us run with perseverance the race that is set before
> us, looking to Jesus the pioneer and perfecter of our
> faith . . . (Heb 12:1b–2a)

Once upon a time I was a runner. It was in the early 1980s, when I was in my mid- thirties. Overweight and easily winded, I started by running up and down the street, then around the block. Slowly, I increased my distance. I still remember the first time I ran for five miles. It was my initiation into the experience of a "runner's high," a feeling of euphoria associated with the release of endorphins in the brain. I was near the intersection of Tampa and Plummer in Northridge, California, running west on Plummer, and the runner's high kicked in. I was euphoric! Exuberant!

What began as an interest became a passion. I ran and ran. As I learned to run farther, I lost weight, and got healthier. I ran a few 5K road races (3.1 miles) and then advanced to 10K road races. (6.2 miles.) Eventually I ran one half-marathon and then another. (13.1 miles.) That's when I began planning for my first marathon. I bought a book and followed the author's step-by-step, mile-by-mile plan. On weekend runs, I slowly increased my distance. By

January of 1984, I did a twenty-mile run. I was ready for my first marathon.

Our family, together with my friend the late Pr. Darcy Jensen, met up for dinner the night before the 1984 Long Beach Marathon. We carbo-loaded at a local Italian restaurant in preparation for the big race. Marathon day was a beautiful Sunday morning. The course was flat and fast. I ran my race and crossed the finish line in under four hours. Darcy finished his race, in less than three hours. (Once we left the starting line, I never saw him again until we met at the finish line.) I had no problems whatsoever though I confess, the last six miles were the hardest. I'd previously run twenty miles, but not twenty-six. It was a grind, but I just kept running.

There are several references to running and races in the New Testament. In addition to the Hebrews 12 passage (see above) St. Paul also uses the images of running, racing, and finish lines in two of his letters. In 2 Timothy, he writes: "I have fought the good fight, I have finished the race; I have kept the faith." Writing to the Corinthians, St. Paul expands the image of runners and races: "Do you not know that in a race the runners all compete, but only one receives the prize? Run in such a way that you may win it. Athletes exercise self-control in all things; they do it to receive a perishable wreath, but we an imperishable one" (1 Cor 9:24–25).

For St. Paul and the anonymous author of the Letter to the Hebrews, running, racing and finish lines were graphic ways of visualizing Christian faith, hope and love. Life in Christ is a journey; according to the Acts of the Apostles, early Christians were actually called people of the Way. Following Jesus, the pioneer and the perfecter of our faith, requires discipline, perseverance, and commitment. Someday, there's a finish line and we'll cross it.

Speaking with my friend Don Post about the recent death of our mutual friend Buzz Kahn, Don imagined Buzz being welcomed to his heavenly home by Don's first wife Nancy who died in 2004. For St. Paul, keeping the faith, running the race, and receiving the winner's "imperishable" wreath were at the heart of his understanding of Christian life and our eternal hope. Life's a marathon; we run to win.

It was Sunday morning at the 1984 Summer Olympics. Members of my family, our friend George Tweten, and I were in the Los Angeles Coliseum, waiting for the finish of the first ever women's Olympic marathon, a road race run through the streets of Los Angeles. Together with millions of television viewers around the world, we watched as Joan Benoit, a runner from Maine, won the first Olympic women's marathon in 2:24:52.

Believe it or not, my most vivid image of the marathon's finish line was *not* Ms. Benoit's win. It was a Swiss runner, named Gabriela Andersen-Scheiss. Ms. Andersen-Scheiss ran into the Coliseum after thirty runners had already finished the marathon ahead of her, but she was in trouble. Suffering from heat exhaustion, Andersen-Schweiss lurched and reeled in an almost drunken gait.

Olympic officials didn't know whether to pull her off the track, or let her continue on her own. As medical officers approached her, Ms. Andersen-Schweiss veered away. The crowd of 70,000, including us, cheered her on. She finished in an agonizingly protracted walk-run. It took five minutes to complete the circuit of the stadium. When she finally crossed the finish line and collapsed into the arms of physicians, the ovation she received was louder than the one for the winner, Joan Benoit.

Ms. Andersen-Schweiss finished thirty-seventh, in a time of 2:48:42. She later said: "The last two kilometers are mainly black; it always seemed longer to the finish than I thought." Lately, I've been thinking about Ms. Andersen-Schweiss' last lap of the 1984 Olympic marathon. As we run the marathon of the coronavirus pandemic, sheltering in place, living with countless losses and waiting for things to return to normal—or to a new normal, or at the very least something other than what feels like the eternal now— it seems longer to the finish line than we thought. As we run the ultra-marathon of dismantling systemic racism, working for justice and equality for all people, it's seems longer to the finish line than we thought. As we persevere in prayer, as we strive to be faithful, hopeful, and loving—as we wait for God's new heaven and new earth, the fullness of God's rule and reign and the healing of the nations— it seems longer to the finish line than we thought.

In preparation for running the 1984 Long Beach Marathon, Darcy and I attended a pre-marathon training clinic. The only thing I remember from that clinic was one of the speakers inviting us to visualize ourselves crossing the finish line. It was his experience that imagining one's self crossing the finish line would draw us forward, reeling us in. As I ran the last six miles of the marathon, the image of the banner above the finish line, and my family and Darcy cheering me on, kept me in the race.

I visualize Jesus, the pioneer and perfecter of our faith, together with what the writer of the book of Hebrews calls "the great cloud of witnesses," cheering us on, and it keeps me in the race. I imagine God's will being done on earth as it is in heaven, and it keeps me in the race. I imagine new heaven and new earth, and no more death and no more mourning and no more crying and no more pain and God wiping away every single one of our tears, and it keeps me in the race.

Psalms and Justice

June 18, 2020

The Psalms are the gymnasium of the soul. (St. Ambrose)

I'VE BEEN PRAYING THE PRAYER poems in the book of Psalms for years. Two formative experiences inspired me to include praying and journaling the Psalms in my spiritual practices. The first was in 1988. I attended a retreat for Lutheran pastors at St. Andrew's Abbey in Valyermo, California. Attending the daily office as monks and guests chanted the Psalms, was a delight. I was inspired and intrigued by this practice and wanted to learn more. In time, I did.

A year later, I attended a one-week class on the Psalms with Eugene H. Peterson at the New College in Berkeley, California. Forming the basis of Pastor Peterson's lectures was material from his soon to be published book, *Answering God: The Psalms As Tools For Prayer*. That week was a turning point for me, Psalms wise. Here's Eugene Peterson on praying the Psalms:

> I ask people to pray the Psalms so that they get exposure
> to the immense range and terrific energies of prayer.
> The church's primary text for teaching men and women
> to pray is the Psalms. Untutored, we tend to think that
> prayer is what good people do when they are doing their
> best. It is not. Inexperienced, we suppose that there must
> be an "insider" language that must be acquired before

God takes us seriously in our prayers. There is not. Prayer is elemental, not advanced, language. It is the means by which our language becomes honest, true, and personal. [1]

The class on the Psalms and the monastic retreat were the catalyst for a new and life-giving practice of praying and journaling the book of Psalms. My practice hasn't changed much over the years; I sit down with a cup of coffee, my Psalter and my journal. I pray and journal five Psalms. As I read and pray, I listen for God's voice. Sometimes the words, phrases and sentences are prayers I offer to God; sometimes the words are promises that reassure me and prepare me for the living of my day. Sometimes the psalm confronts me with my sin and leads me to confession; sometimes the words soothe and console me. Sometimes the verses invite rest and refreshment. The words of lament, praise, comfort, judgment, gratitude, and anger help me express the full range of my emotions. The Psalms have served this purpose for God's people for 3,000 years.

Last Sunday morning I sat down with my Psalter, a cup of coffee and my journal, and prayed and wrote notes on Psalms 7–11. Here are some notes from my journal:

> Lord God, you are my haven . . . Put an end to evil; uphold what is good. (Psalm 7) Lord, our God, the whole world tells the greatness of your name. I see your handiwork in the heavens: the moon and stars you set in place. (Psalm 8) With a heart full of thanks, I proclaim your wonders, God. You are my joy; my delight. Defend the oppressed; fortify them in times of trouble. God avenges the poor and never neglects their cries. The Lord never lets their hope die. (Psalm 9) Lord where are you when we need you? Arise God and act; do not ignore the weak. Lord, hear the longing of the poor, listen to their every word, and give them heart. Then the poor and oppressed will gain justice and tyrants lose their power. (Psalm 10) When the world falls apart, what can the good hope to

---

1. Peterson, "Listen Yahweh" 38.

do? The Lord loves justice; the just will see God's face
(Psalm 11).

Praying five Psalms, I was encouraged by words of praise and
joy, and, reminded of God's commitment to the poor, oppressed
and troubled. The promise and reassurance that the Lord never
neglects the cries of the poor and never lets their hope die, bears
witness to the teachings of Jewish and Christian Holy Scriptures
about God's zeal for justice. On Monday, our nephew Tim Hoiland
posted "Psalms of Justice," an article by W. David O. Taylor, on
Twitter. Dr. Taylor writes that it wasn't until he began to study
the Psalms that he discovered "the centrality of justice to faithful
Christian living. The Bible changed my mind, and it changed how
I saw the world around me." He continues:

> The fact that injustices occur every day will be obvious to
> anyone who follows the news. Injustices happen to indi-
> viduals, mar institutions, and befall entire people groups.
> The killing of George Floyd was a high-profile tipping
> point of sorts in our awareness of grievous injustice.
> But terrible injustices occur each day, in each commu-
> nity, far removed from the headlines. For the psalmists,
> such a world is all too familiar, and they pray repeatedly
> for justice because they understand that a world full of
> broken humans and powers and principalities generates
> injustice everywhere and always . . . When we look to
> the Psalms—which functioned as Jesus' prayer book and
> have functioned for 2,000 years as the church's official
> hymnbook, teaching Christians how to talk to God and
> hear from God—we discover that there is no true wor-
> ship, faithful prayer, or genuine faith that neglects justice.
> No true account of God makes justice an afterthought to
> his redemptive work in the world. This is decidedly good
> news for our fractured world. [2]

Our fractured, pandemic ridden, troubled and conflicted
world needs all the good news it can get and all the justice we can
offer. Friends in Christ: we are baptized, called and sent, to bear

2. Taylor, "Psalms of Justice."

witness to God's love for justice. The liturgy for the Sacrament of Holy Baptism includes the charge to all the baptized: "Proclaim Christ through word and deed, care for others and the world God made and work for justice and peace." Doing justice, loving mercy, and walking humbly with God is at the heart of our life together and our practice of loving our neighbors as ourselves.

Care of the Sick Must Rank
Above and Before All Else

June 25, 2020

Care of the sick must rank above and before all else
so that they may truly be served as Christ who said, "I
was sick and you visited me." (The Rule of St. Benedict:
Chapter 36, "The Sick")

OUR THREE-YEAR OLD SON ANDERS was sick and hospitalized. His
pediatrician had told us to bring him to the emergency room; he
was subsequently admitted to the hospital. What I remember most
about that experience—besides my concern for his health and
well-being—was the realization that with our son in the hospital,
our family's center of gravity shifted from our home to his hospital room. That's where our family life was. Home wasn't a place;
home was our family, and our love for each other. It was a powerful
learning experience for me, one I've never forgotten.

More than four months into the coronavirus pandemic, it
feels like the center of gravity is constantly shifting. I don't know
anyone anywhere whose life hasn't been impacted by the pandemic. We continue to cancel travel plans, reschedule weddings,
postpone funerals, shelter in place, wear masks, social distance
and strive to stay safe and healthy. It seems like we've all been

deputized as volunteer public health workers. When I wear a mask for you and you wear a mask for me, we dramatically reduce our risks for getting COVID-19.

Conversely, when we fail to practice these common-sense measures, we increase the risks and the number of cases of CO-VID-19. State health officials reported 516 new coronavirus infections in Washington on Tuesday as well as eight additional deaths. This brings the state's totals to 29,386 cases and 1,284 deaths. Until there is a new vaccine, the best practice for reducing risk and for saving lives is using the tools that work.

Over fifteen hundred years ago, Benedict of Nursia founded a monastery at Monte Cassino, Italy, where he wrote his rule for living in Christian community. The Rule of St. Benedict changed the face of Christianity in Western Europe and has impacted the lives of millions of Christians over the centuries. Benedict's rule (think of it as guide for life together in Christ) is part of the wisdom tradition in Christianity and is anchored in Holy Scriptures. In chapter 36 of the rule, Benedict states unequivocally that, "Care of the sick must rank above and before all else so that they may truly be served as Christ who said, 'I was sick and you visited me.'" Benedict taught that the prioress or the abbot "should be extremely careful that they (the sick) suffer no neglect."[1]

I remember the first time I read chapter 36. I'd been to seminary; I'd been a pastor for many years. I knew a thing or two about the importance of pastoral care and counsel for people who are sick and dying, but I was not prepared for Benedict's teaching that care of the sick "ranked above and before all else." No one had ever told me that before. On countless occasions I'd dropped everything and sped to the hospital when church members had heart attacks, strokes or other emergencies. But the thought that care of the sick was *always* to rank above and before all else was new.

This should come as no surprise. Care of the sick was at the heart of the ministry of Jesus, and the mission he entrusted to his disciples. According to the Gospel of Matthew, Jesus, "Summoned his twelve disciples and gave them authority over unclean spirits,

1. Chittister, *The Rule of St. Benedict: Insights for the Ages*, 113.

to cast them out, and to cure every disease and every sickness." (Matt 10:1) His marching orders included instructions to proclaim the good news, announce that the kingdom of heaven has come near, and cure the sick. As I think about our current moment, I believe God is calling each one of us, to be ambassadors of God's shalom, wholeness, and peace. Putting our neighbor first and using the tools that can save lives is a faithful way to love Christ who is present to us in our neighbors.

Prayer and action bear witness to the love of God and the tender mercies of Jesus, the great physician. As we offer our prayers for those who are sick from COVID-19 and other diseases and conditions, I invite you to also offer prayers for healthcare workers as well. Here is a prayer for health care providers from *Evangelical Lutheran Worship*:

> Merciful God, your healing power is everywhere about us. Strengthen those who work among the sick; give them courage and confidence in all they do. Encourage them when their efforts seem futile or when death prevails. Increase their trust in your power even to overcome death and pain and crying. May they be thankful for every sign of health you give, and humble before the mystery of your healing grace; through Jesus Christ our Lord. Amen.[2]

---

2. *Evangelical Lutheran Worship*, 85.

Powerless

July 2, 2020

Jesus got into the boat; his disciples followed him. A
windstorm arose on the sea, so great that the boat was
being swamped by the waves; but Jesus was asleep. The
disciples went and woke him up, saying, "Lord, save us!
We are perishing!" And he said to them, "Why are you
afraid, you of little faith?" Then Jesus got up and rebuked
the winds and the sea; and there was a dead calm.

(Matt 8:23–26)

IT WAS A BEAUTIFUL SUN-SPLASHED, blue sky summer day at Zuma
Beach in Malibu, California. As a young Southern Californian, the
beach was my home away from home. I couldn't get enough of it.
On this particular afternoon, several of my friends and I waded
into the ocean for a swim and some body surfing. At some point,
we realized we'd drifted out beyond where the waves were breaking. We tried to swim back to shore, but we were powerless against
the force of the current. No matter how hard we swam, the tide
kept pulling us out.

Fortunately, some Los Angeles County lifeguards saw us and
swam to our rescue. Using ring buoys and rescue tubes they were
able to swim us safely back to shore. As we walked across the hot

sand from the water's edge, I was embarrassed by the spectators and wanted to run for cover. I was a surfer, an experienced swimmer, and I was mortified by the attention and humiliated by my experience of powerlessness. I couldn't save myself; I had to be rescued.

Getting caught in a rip tide is a graphic image for the experience of powerlessness. Losing control, not being able to have everything work out the way I want, falling short of goals and desired outcomes is nothing new. It's how things are. It's a fact of life and a universal human experience. Our ancestors of every time and place have had to contend with the reality that humans are at times powerless in the face of situations and circumstances beyond our control. Our forbears contended with famines, catastrophes, and natural disasters. My grandparents lived through two world wars, the 1918 influenza pandemic, the Great Depression, and the social upheavals of the 1960s.

What's distinctive about the current moment is that we are experiencing loss of control to a degree that is unprecedented for most of us alive today. Yes, there are aspects of my life over which I am *not* powerless. For example, I can avoid getting COVID-19 by sheltering in place, social distancing, wearing a mask in public, and avoiding large gatherings. However, the number of things that are out of my control is growing. We are living in the middle of a resurgence of the pandemic that has impacted our daily lives, relationships, work, and the economy. There are things that we can do to avoid getting COVID-19 or giving it to others, but what others choose to do or not do is out of our control.

The disciples of Jesus knew a thing or two about powerlessness. In a boat on the sea, a windstorm came up and the waves swamped the boat. Jesus was fast asleep. The disciples panicked; their fear got the better of them and they woke Jesus up pleading with him to save them— after all, they were perishing! Three times in the Gospel of Matthew, Jesus calls out the disciples on their "little faith." This is just one of them. Immobilized by their fear, they were incapable of trusting in God's faithfulness. Turning to

Jesus, they pleaded for deliverance and Jesus delivered – big time! He rebuked the winds and the sea, and there was dead calm.

Some years ago, we attended a Gymanfa Ganu (a Welsh festival of sacred hymns sung in four-part harmony) in Bellevue, Washington. Mary Morris Mergenthal, the song leader, introduced the gathering to a hymn called, "In the Waves and Mighty Waters." In 1877, Ms. Mergenthan told us, five miners were trapped in a mine in South Wales for eight days. They had no food. They had no way to know if or when they'd be rescued. They kept sane by singing "In the Waves and Mighty Waters." This is what they sang:

> In the mighty waters and waves
> There is no one to hold my head
> But my beloved Jesus who died upon the cross
> He is the friend in the river of death
> Holding my head above the wave
> His face makes me sing in this deep river. [1]

The miners were rescued eight days later after 218 hours without food or clean water. The miners who rescued them hacked their way through a 114-foot, barrier of coal. In the e-mail that Ms. Mergenthal sent me in response to my request for this story, she closed with these words: "I hope that keeps your interest in Welsh hymnody alive. But more importantly, I hope it nourishes your faith in Jesus, who holds us as the waters of life rise." It sure does.

---

1. "In the Waves of the Mighty Waters" (Public Domain).

Joy
July 8, 2020

I have said these things to you so that my joy may be in
you, and that your joy may be complete. (John 15:11)

SOMETIMES I EMAIL MY SAMMAMISH Hills pastoral letters to family and friends. After reading last week's letter, Louise Evenson
wrote back saying:

> This week, on a Zoom with friends, I asked them to think
> of how they'd found joy in their lives that week. Every-
> thing changed in the conversation . . . smiles, stories, a
> lighter feeling. Without being Pollyanna, I think this is
> a time of testing our ability to find hope and joy while
> in isolation. Thankfully, it's the small things . . . a visit
> to Underwood Farms for our weekly produce, a fourth
> of July BBQ, listening to John Williams' arrangement of
> 'Summon the Heroes,' (Composed for the 1996 Olympic
> Games in Atlanta, Georgia) that bring us joy. There are
> so many signs and people of hope.[1]

I think Louise is right. Yesterday, during our weekly Zoom
prayer gathering, I read Louise's email to our group and invited
participants to share what brought them joy the previous week.

---

1. Louise Evenson, *Personal Correspondence.*

What stood out for me was that the things that brought us joy weren't *things* at all; no one talked about their newest purchase or their favorite possession. We talked about beautiful days (and nights) and the wonders of creation. We talked about time with others and staying connected to family and friends. We talked about all the foods we enjoy. (More than one of us rejoiced in our love for Italian food!)

Our Zoom experience was almost identical to Louise's; we laughed, we joked and we savored wonder. There was a lighter, relaxed feeling, as we spoke with each other. Louise's invitation to her friends felt like a wakeup call to me. I want to be vigilant and informed about what is going on locally, nationally and globally regarding the coronavirus pandemic and the urgency of righting the wrongs of racism and injustice. I also want and need to be attentive to the daily blessings of joy, wonder and grace..

The gospel truth is that joy is a gift, pure and simple. What's more, when it comes to joy, no one gets preferential treatment. Our status, success, or prosperity do not guarantee joy. The poorest of the poor can be joyful. And that's not all; adversity, calamity, troubles, and trials needn't rob us of our joy. St. James writes: "My brothers and sisters, whenever you face trials of any kind, consider it nothing but joy, because you know that the testing of your faith produces endurance, and let endurance have its full effect, so that you may be mature and complete, lacking in nothing." (1:2).

These words seem counter-intuitive, especially in the current moment, but they ring true as I remember joy-filled Christians I've met in Rwanda, China and Peru. Our global sisters and brothers in Christ teach us that the joy of the Lord is our strength, inviting us to trust in God's faithfulness, no matter what.

What's joy? My *Webster's Dictionary* says joy is a noun: "Joy is a very glad feeling; happiness; great pleasure; delight. Joy is anything causing this feeling. Joy is the expression of this feeling." This Webster's definition is good, as far as it goes, but I think joy is more and deeper than a feeling or an emotion. St. Paul, writing about the generosity of the churches of Macedonia in his second letter to the Corinthians wrote: "During a severe ordeal of affliction, their [the Macedonians'] abundant joy and their extreme poverty, have overflowed in a wealth of generosity on their part" (8:2). The seeds of God's grace and peace take root in our hearts and grow the gift of joy.

Circumstances, situations, afflictions, severe ordeals, or pandemics needn't compromise our joy. In his book, *Wishful Thinking,* Frederick Buechner writes:

> In the gospel of John, Jesus sums up pretty much everything by saying, 'These things I have spoken to you, that my joy may be in you and that your joy may be full.' Happiness turns up more or less where you'd expect it to: In a good marriage, a rewarding job, or a pleasant vacation. Joy, on the other hand, is as notoriously unpredictable as the one who bequeaths it. [2]

---

2. Buechner, *Wishful Thinking,* 47.

The Mercy Rule

July 12, 2020

Blessed are the merciful, for they will receive mercy.
(Matt 5:7)

IT WAS JULY 1990, AND we were waiting in the boarding area at Los Angeles International Airport for our sons Anders and Soren to board a flight to Seattle to visit their grandparents. I noticed a group of men waiting with us. I noticed them because they appeared to be athletes but they weren't decked out in running suits or brand name athletic apparel; a lot of them were sporting cowboy hats and all of them were speaking Russian. Turns out they were the Soviet Union's baseball team en route to Seattle, Washington, for the Goodwill Games.

On Thursday, July 26, 1990, the first game of the Goodwill Games baseball tournament featured the Soviet Union's baseball team playing the American baseball team. According to Mike Penner, a staff writer for the *Los Angeles Times*, the tournament planners had decreed that there would be a ten-run mercy rule, "once Thursday's game reached the seventh inning." (The mercy rule terminates a game early if one of the two teams has taken a substantial lead, considered to be insurmountable.)

Mr. Penner wrote: "After 6 ½ innings at Tacoma's Cheney Stadium, the Soviets ended their primer in that intriguing American exercise known as baseball. The final score was United States 17, Soviet Union 0." [1] The *Times* headline read: "Goodwill Games Score: U.S. 17, Soviet Union 0, Have Mercy." I read Mr. Penner's reporting the morning following the game with great interest as I remembered the youthful exuberance of the Soviet baseball players at the airport.

By the way, in case you didn't know, there's no mercy rule in Major League Baseball. On August 22, 2007 the Texas Rangers beat the Baltimore Orioles by a score of 30–3 setting a modern-era record for most runs in a single game. Freddie Bynum, who played shortstop and leftfield for the Orioles that day, was quoted in *Sports Illustrated* saying, "You're asking like, man, do they have a mercy rule? You know there ain't, but you're hoping for one."[2]

Mercy. What a word. What a wonder. I love the sound of the word mercy. I love the meaning of the word mercy. According to the *Merriman-Webster* dictionary, mercy is, "compassion or forbearance shown especially to an offender or to one subject to one's power." There is no counting all the times I've been on the receiving end of God's mercy, not to mention the mercy of others; I hope the number of times I've shown mercy equals—or, better yet, exceeds—all the times people have been merciful to me.

One of my favorite Bible verses is in the book of Lamentations, a heart- rending account of the destruction of Jerusalem by the Babylonians in 587 BC. A book of lament and suffering written out of the Hebrew people's exile experience, the poet finds light and hope in the daily darkness of pain and loss: "The steadfast love of the Lord never ceases, his mercies never come to an end; they are new every morning; great is your faithfulness" (Lam 3:23).

In the midst of our losses, doubts, fears and worries, the promise of God's steadfast love, faithfulness, and daily, endless mercies, is a healing balm and a beacon of hope for the living of our days. It's also a daily reminder to be a mercy giver.

1. Penner, *Los Angeles Times,* July 27, 1990.
2. Tayler, *Sports Illustrated,* August 22, 2017.

"Mercy is all about unfairness," according to *Crazy Talk: A Not So Stuffy Dictionary of Theological Terms*, edited by Rolf A. Jacobson.

> God is merciful. God's mercy is all about unfairness. If God treated us as fairness demanded, we'd be in some serious trouble . . . If God remembered it against us every time we worshipped our idols of money, career, family, war, or sex, we'd be forgotten forever (so to speak). If God brought charges against us each time we ignored the widow or orphan, we'd be serving multiple eternal life sentences (concurrently). But God isn't fair. God is mercy. Mercy is who God is. Because of God's mercy, we can, "return to the Lord, our God, for he is gracious and merciful, slow to anger, and abounding in steadfast love." (Joel 2:23) [3]

In the Sermon on the Mount, Jesus said, "Blessed are the merciful" (Matt 5:7). If that's not a call to sharing the gifts of God's love and grace with others, I don't know what is. I recently realized that I sometimes get confused about the words of Micah 6:8, which reads "What does the Lord require of you but to do justice, and to love kindness, and to walk humbly with your God?" Sometimes I say or write, "do justice, love *mercy*, and walk humbly with God . . . " The more I think about it, the more I wonder: What's the difference? If you're treating me with kindness or mercy, and/or if I am being kind and merciful to you, are we actually going to call a time out and try to figure out if we're being kind or merciful? I don't think so..

A few weeks ago, Ann and I watched "Tender Mercies," the 1983 film starring Robert Duvall (as Mac Sledge) and Tess Harper (as Rosa Lee.) Mac is a washed-up country singer who quits drinking and starts writing songs again thanks to the love of his new wife Rosa and her young son, Sonny. I love the line that gives the film its name. Rosa Lee and Mac are visiting on the front porch after Mac's former manager has informed him that one of his newly written songs "is no good." Mac's anger is tempered by Rosa Lee's

---

3. Jacobson, *Crazy Talk*, 114–115.

kindness and grace as she tells Mac: "Every night when I say my prayers and thank the Lord for his blessings and his tender mercies to me, you and Sonny, head the list." Mac replies, "Thank you." [4]

4. Beresford, Bruce, director, 1983. *Tender Mercies*. Universal Pictures.

Anger Management

July 16, 2020

Be angry but do not sin; do not let the sun go down on
your anger. (Eph 4:26)

IT'S A BEAUTIFUL DAY IN the neighborhood. I've just come in from
working in the yard. I'm sitting at one of my favorite writing spots,
listening to birdsong with a mug of hot tea on the table beside me.
Right here, right now, in this perfectly lovely moment, all is right
with the world. I am at peace. If I turn on the television or the
radio, chances are my temporary bliss will be disrupted. I'll hear or
read some bad news. Some of the bad news may annoy me, distress
me, or even make me angry. Thankfully, all is well, for now.

I've been thinking about anger. I'd rather not, but I can't help
it. Sometimes I think about my own anger. Sometimes I think
about the anger of others. Over the years, I've learned to manage
my anger, but I can't manage anyone else's. Too late in life I realized
that as troubled as I am by my own feelings of anger, it doesn't
compare to my fear of the anger of others. For too many years I
tried (mostly in vain) to manage other people's anger by being a
conflict avoiding people pleaser. Sometimes it worked; most of
the time it didn't. A turning point for me was the realization that
conflict avoidance made me miserable, so I wondered, "Why not

experiment with the misery of conflict *engagement*?" It didn't necessarily change outcomes, but it was liberating nevertheless.

Evagrius Ponticus, a fourth century Christian monk, compiled a list of eight common sins to help people be aware of them and guard against them. In the sixth century, Pope Gregory I reduced the list to seven, providing us with what we now refer to as the seven deadly sins: sloth, anger, envy, pride, lust, gluttony, and greed. In her book, *Amazing Grace: A Vocabulary of Faith*, Kathleen Norris writes that Evagrius believed God gave us anger as a gift so that we might fight against true evil. However, Evagrius says, "We sin with anger when we misapply it and use it against other people." Ms. Norris writes, "Christian monks believed that human anger is our biggest obstacle to love. To become mindful of one's anger was seen as an essential but difficult task."[1]

St. Paul's anger advice is helpful. On the one hand, he affirms and acknowledges that anger is a given; on the other hand, he cautions us to not let our anger get the better of us. "Be angry but do not sin," he writes. Then, on the off chance that I might not understand, he adds a sobering word of warning: "Do not let the sun set on your anger." (Eph 4:26). In other words, acknowledge your anger; attend to your anger; deal with your anger. Don't let it fester; don't let it take root and turn into bitterness. Unbridled, my anger can rip and tear and hurt and wound. Managed, my anger is a way to express my hurt, disappointment, and even righteous indignation at evils perpetrated on people who are vulnerable and marginalized. Righteous anger has its place (see Jesus' cleansing of the temple in John 2:13–15). Out of control anger is harmful, sinful, and can even be abusive.

What do we do with our anger? How do we manage it? As we make our way through these difficult and trying times, Mayo Clinic's "10 Tips to Tame Your Temper" is helpful.

> Anger Management: 10 Tips to Tame Your Temper (The Mayo Clinic)
> Do you fume when someone cuts you off in traffic?
> Does your blood pressure rocket when your child refuses

---

1. Norris, *Amazing Grace*, 126–127.

to cooperate? Anger is a normal and even healthy emotion — but it's important to deal with it in a positive way. Ready to get your anger under control? Start by considering these 10 anger management tips.

1. Think before you speak: Take a few moments to collect your thoughts before saying anything — and allow others involved in the situation to do the same.

2. Once you're calm, express your anger: As soon as you're thinking clearly, express your frustration in an assertive but non-confrontational way.

3. Get some exercise: Physical activity can help reduce stress that can cause you to become angry.

4. Take a timeout: Timeouts aren't just for kids. Give yourself short breaks during times of the day that tend to be stressful.

5. Identify possible solutions: Instead of focusing on what made you mad, work on resolving the issue at hand.

6. Stick with 'I' statements: To avoid criticizing or placing blame — which might only increase tension — use "I" statements to describe the problem. Be respectful and specific.

7. Don't hold a grudge: If you allow anger and other negative feelings to crowd out positive feelings, you might find yourself swallowed up by your own bitterness or sense of injustice. But if you can forgive someone who angered you, you might both learn from the situation and strengthen your relationship.

8. Use humor to release tension: Lightening up can help diffuse tension. Use humor to help you face what's making you angry and, possibly, any unrealistic expectations you have for how things should go.

9. Practice relaxation skills: When your temper flares, put relaxation skills to work.

10. Know when to seek help: Learning to control anger is a challenge for everyone at times. Seek help for anger issues if your anger seems out of control, causes you to do things you regret or hurts those around you. [2]

---

2. Mayo Clinic Staff, "Anger Management: 10 Tips To Tame Your Anger."

Birth of a Nation, My Grandmother, and a John Lewis Forgiveness Story

July 30, 2020

Jesus said, "If you forgive others their trespasses, your heavenly Father will also forgive you; but if you do not forgive others, neither will your Father forgive your trespasses. (Matt 6:14–15)

WHEN SHE DIED IN DECEMBER 2001, my step grandmother, Phoebe Rosenfeld, (a.k.a. Mary Wynn) was the last surviving (uncredited) cast member of D.W. Griffith's Civil War epic, *Birth of a Nation* (1915). An offensive and blatantly racist film, based on Thomas Dixon's 1905 novel, *The Clansman, Birth of a Nation's* release in 1915 generated widespread controversy and sparked the 1920s revival of the Ku Klux Klan. My grandmother was a gracious and kind person whom I loved dearly. I was proud of her brief career in the early days of motion pictures, though I had never seen *Birth of a Nation* and knew next to nothing about its content or her part in the film.

In 2015, I read *The Birth of a Nation: How a Legendary Filmmaker and a Crusading Editor Reignited America's Civil War*, Dick Lehr's book about the film, director D.W. Griffith and Monroe Trotter, the "crusading editor" of the book's title. Mr. Trotter, the first Black man to attend Harvard, was appalled by *Birth of a Nation* and organized mass demonstrations (together with the newly formed NAACP) in opposition to the film. Having read Mr. Lehr's book, I thought it was time for me to view this three-hour film. Though I had learned a lot about it by reading Mr. Lehr's book, I was stunned by my visceral reaction to the movie.

As I watched the film I was shocked, embarrassed and ashamed. I was repulsed by the film's bigoted portrayal of Black Americans and its glorification of the KKK and white supremacy. My feelings of embarrassment and shame were exacerbated by the experience of sitting in a Bellevue, Washington, movie theatre three years later watching Spike Lee's 2018 film, *BlacKkKlansman*, which included the scene from *Birth of a Nation* that my grandmother appeared in. Sitting alone in the theater I felt like the skeletons were tumbling out of the family closet. I didn't know what to think but I sure knew what I was feeling: fear. I was afraid of what people would think of me, or my family, if they knew that my beloved grandmother was a cast member of this disgraceful film.

According to her obituary, grandmother Phoebe's appearance in *Birth of a Nation* was brief, but pivotal.

> In the few minutes of her screen appearance, Phoebe and a young playmate cover themselves with sheets and jump out of concealment in some bushes to frighten a group of black children walking along a country road. In the scene, the frightened and fleeing children were observed by the film's protagonist the Little Colonel. This became his inspiration for garbing his newly formed gang of avengers, the infamous Ku Klux Klan.

I never discussed her appearance in *Birth of a Nation* with my grandmother. I don't know what she thought about it let alone how she felt, but I know that I grieve the fact that the impact of this film on the lives of Black Americans was horrific and incalculable.

In a recent blog post for the Center for Courage and Renewal, founder Dr. Parker Palmer shared a story about his personal experience with the late congressman and civil rights activist, John Lewis, who recently died on July 17, 2020. Dr. Palmer writes that his autographed copy of Mr. Lewis' memoir, *Walking with the Wind*, is one of his most precious possessions. In 2011, Dr. Palmer and his wife spent three days with John Lewis on his annual 2011 Civil Rights Pilgrimage, "which ended with a memorial march across the Edmund Pettus Bridge in Selma, Alabama, on the 48th anniversary of Bloody Sunday." Mr. Palmer writes:

> Walking behind a 71-year-old John Lewis to commemorate the historic march he led at age 24 was a lesson in commitment and courage that will always be with me. After the march, we boarded a bus from Selma back to the Montgomery, Alabama Airport, and found ourselves sitting behind John Lewis and his seatmate. As the bus sped thru a countryside that had been a KKK killing ground, we heard Lewis tell a story that later went public.
>
> In 1961, Lewis (age 21) and two other Freedom Riders were beaten and bloodied by a gang of young white men at a Greyhound bus terminal in Rock Hill, South Carolina. Forty-eight years later, in 2009, a man about Lewis' age, walked into Congressman Lewis' Capitol Hill office with his son. "I'm Elwin Wilson," the man said. "I'm one of the men who beat you in Rock Hill, back when I belonged to the KKK. I've come to seek your forgiveness." Lewis forgave Wilson without hesitation. Then, said Lewis, "He started crying, his son started crying, and I started crying. Then we talked."
>
> Their talking continued, sometimes in public, until Wilson died in 2013. At that time, Lewis commented, "Elwin Wilson told me he wanted to be right when he met his Maker, and I believe he accomplished what he set out to do. He's the only person who has ever apologized to me." When I heard Lewis tell this story in March of 2011, he ended with a line I can hear him say to this day. After recounting Wilson's visit to his office, he fell silent as he looked out the window of that speeding bus. Then he said, very quietly, "People can change. People can change." When I heard him speak those words, it filled me with hope—not just for them—but also for me. Personal change takes the humility to admit that one was wrong, a willingness to bear the weight of one's wrongs,

and the courage to try to right them. So every day, I need to ask myself, "What about me? Do I have the guts to confess my wrongs and take corrective action?"[1]

I am grateful to God for John Lewis and I pray that as the nation celebrates his life and legacy that we will be inspired to follow his devotion to the teachings of Jesus and offer the gift of forgiveness to others. As I consider the ongoing challenges of life during the pandemic, I am thankful to God for every act of love, mercy, and forgiveness and the wonderful gospel truth that people can change.

A sobering local history postscript: On Sunday, July 26, 1924, Issaquah, Washington was the sight of the largest Ku Klux Klan gathering in Washington state history. According to Sherry Grindeland's July 25, 1997 *Seattle Times* article, "Estimates of the crowd that met in the summer of 1924 in what is now downtown Issaquah ranged from 20,000 to 55,000. 'Deputies who clicked off the vehicles on hand counters said there were four to five people per car', according to the August 1, 1924 edition of The Issaquah Press." Ms. Grindeland writes:

> That would put the crowd somewhere between 44,000 and 55,000, people although some historians estimate the gathering was about 20,000. According to historians Joe Peterson and Lucile McDonald, it wasn't unusual for a small town like Issaquah to have an active Klan. The group officially organized nationally in 1915 with an agenda to keep the United States for white, American born Protestants. The Klan went on to terrorize minorities, especially African Americans, as it organized public whippings and lynching's.[2]

1. Palmer, "It's One of My Most Treasured Possessions."
2. Grindeland, "The Day The Klan Came To Town."

Dear Concerned

August 6, 2020

As God's chosen ones, holy and beloved, clothe yourselves with compassion, kindness, humility, meekness and patience. (Col 3:12)

Dear Amy: My husband of two years recently became interested in exploring Christianity. He went to church as a child, but stopped going as a teen. He is now very concerned about what will happen after he dies. He says he wants to find "peace." I have no interest in going with him. Concerned Wife. ("Ask Amy" *Seattle Times*, August 2, 2020)

Let's call them Mary and John (not their real names). I knew them in another state in another century. Mary and John had grown up in families that practiced different religions. One was a traditional Christian faith, the other, a centuries old religion practiced in the Middle East. By the time Mary and John met and married, neither one of them was practicing their religions. In spite of the fact that they were raised in very different faith traditions, their non-practice meant their religious differences were a non-issue. Until something (actually, someone) changed.

What changed was that John had a dramatic and life changing conversion experience. Mary didn't see it coming and was very distressed as she considered her options. John wanted her to join him in his new Christian faith and attend worship with him. He was hoping and praying that she would become a Christian. She wasn't interested. The three of us met several times and worked to identify the issues that needed to be addressed. Eventually, we lost track of each other and I have no idea what happened to John and Mary or their marriage. The ideal solution would have been for Mary and John to unconditionally love each other and accept, embrace, and even celebrate their differences.

I thought about Mary and John after reading last Sunday's "Ask Amy" column in the *Seattle Times*. The headline got my attention big time: "Wife Does Not Want to Join Husband As He Makes His Way Back to Church." The concerned wife was neither interested in going to worship with her husband nor was she, "comfortable participating in organized religion." Her question to Amy was sobering: "Do I need to be a part of this? I feel like I will hate every minute of it and become resentful. But if I don't go, will it ruin our marriage?"

Amy's wise and forthright advice was impressive. She identified the primary issues and counseled the concerned wife with thoughtful compassion.

> Dear Concerned: Your marriage shouldn't be contingent on you being forced to worship with your husband. I do suggest you remain open to hearing about his experience—ask him how the service went and what the topic of the sermon was, and perhaps attend special holiday services if he seems eager to share them with you."

Amy was realistic in addressing the possible impacts of the husband's attending church.

> The churchgoing experience will bring your husband into a belief system, as well as a new social system. Any time anyone forms new relationships it could place a strain on the marriage, but the alternative (shadowing

him out of fear that the marriage will be threatened) is a non-starter. [1]

What surprised me was Amy's sense of how the outcome of the husband's churchgoing could change him for the better:

> If he starts attending Bible study and joins church-centered social groups, you will discover that church activities are time consuming. This might negatively affect your relationship, but his faith could also lead him to a more loving, compassionate, and peaceful place.

I wish I'd had a copy of Amy's column to share with Mary and John way back when. I think her counsel would have been helpful.

People who are loving and compassionate thanks to the good news of God's grace in Jesus Christ crucified and risen is what the church is *for*; it's why we're *here*. Our worship, study, service, fellowship, prayers, mutual encouragement—any and everything we do—is dedicated to creating opportunities and encounters (personal or virtual) where people can experience God's grace and then, forgiven and free, are empowered and equipped to share God's love with others.

One of my favorite Bible texts is Col 3:12–17. Paul is writing about the gift of life together in Christian community. I love the *Message* translation of these verses and always suggest this reading to couples preparing for their weddings:

> So, chosen by God for this new life of love, dress in the wardrobe God picked out for you: compassion, kindness, humility, quiet strength, discipline. Be even-tempered, content with second place, quick to forgive an offense. Forgive as quickly and completely as the Master forgave you. And regardless of what else you put on, wear love. It's your basic, all-purpose garment. Never be without it.

Last weekend Ann and I watched "Ball of Fire," a 1941 screwball comedy starring Gary Cooper and Barbara Stanwyck. The film is the story of a group of academics holed up in a mansion in

---

1. Dickinson, "Wife Does Not Want to Join Husband As He Makes His Way Back to Church."

Manhattan working on a new encyclopedia. Soliciting help for his article on American slang (zigzag, hunky dory, skedaddle) Professor Bertram Potts (played by Gary Cooper) recruits a rogue's gallery of characters to provide advice and counsel on the current state of slang. After a chance encounter with the nightclub performer Sugarpuss O'Shea (played by Barbary Stanwyck) Professor Potts welcomes Ms. O'Shea into his impromptu American slang advisory council. There are subplots a plenty, which I will refrain from chronicling other than to reveal that Professor Potts falls in love with Sugarpuss O'Shea. On the eve of their nuptials, Potts gets some wise counsel from Professor Robinson, the only one of his fellow scholars who was ever married. "Patience and tenderness are the most important things," he says softly.[2]

Patience, tenderness, compassion, love, and peace are integral to healthy, functional marriages and families. Now more than ever, these virtues and practices are essential to our life together as a congregation, and to our households, neighborhoods, schools and workplaces (both virtual and physical), as well as our nation and our world.

---

2. Hawks, Howard, director. 1941 *Ball of Fire*. Samuel Goldwyn Productions.

Storms

August 13, 2020

On that day, when evening had come, Jesus said to
the disciples, "Let us go across to the other side." And
leaving the crowd behind, they took him with them in
the boat, just as he was. Other boats were with him. A
great windstorm arose, and the waves beat into the boat,
so that the boat was already being swamped. But Jesus
was in the stern, asleep on the cushion; and they woke
him and said to him, "Teacher, do you not care that we
are perishing? He woke up and rebuked the wind, and
said to the sea, "Peace! Be still!" Then the wind ceased,
and there was a dead calm. Jesus said to them, "Why
are you afraid? Have you still no faith?" And they were
filled with great awe and said to one another, "Who
then is this, that even the wind and sea obey him?"
(Mark 4:35–41)

I DON'T KNOW ABOUT YOU, but I think that if I would have been
one of the disciples in the boat with Jesus that evening, I might
have figured there was nothing to worry about. I mean stop and
think about it: Jesus says, "Let's go across to the other side." And

so we leave the crowd behind. Our boat, with Jesus resting in the stern, makes its way with other boats across the water. What could go wrong? After all, Jesus is sleeping. He's not worried, anxious, or fretting about anything so why should we?

As a youngster, my earliest visual image of Jesus was formed by a framed print of the painting *Christ Our Pilot,* by Warner Sallman that hung on a wall in my bedroom. It portrayed a young man in a bright red shirt at the wheel of a ship, with Jesus standing behind him. In the picture, the wheel is big, the sky is stormy, and Jesus (a pretty tall Jesus I might add) is peering over the shoulder of the young man, guiding him, directing him, and pointing the way. That image always gave me a sense of peace, a sense that I was not alone, a sense that Jesus was with me guiding me through the storm, whatever the storm might be.

I have rarely felt so overwhelmed, storm tossed or distressed that I didn't also feel (if and when I *remembered*) that Jesus was there to guide me to the other side of whatever chaos or confusion, from without or within, I was enduring. My problem is that when I *forget* that I am not alone, I am at risk to worry, fear, and even panic about all manner of maladies and mishaps. Like the disciples, we are making our way with Jesus. The storms come up and our hearts sink. The waves surge and toss and beat against the little boats of our lives. Troubles, trials, and tumults, rise up and batter us and soak our hearts. As our faith flounders, we wonder, like the disciples, "Good God, do you not care that we are perishing?"

Day by day we are making our way with Jesus and there are days when storms are brewing. We hang on for dear life to the promises and presence of Jesus even as we are buffeted by sin, longsuffering, sickness, injustice, discouragement, and problems a plenty. Like the disciples, we wonder if God cares. Now and then, by God's grace, we go ahead and trust God in spite of appearances. Sadly, more often than any of us would care to admit, we are forgetful when it comes to God's faithfulness. Our forgetfulness leads to faithlessness.

When the disciples roused Jesus from his rest, he rebuked the wind and stilled the storm-tossed seas; the wind ceased and there was dead calm. The disciples had asked Jesus if he cared that they were perishing. Now Jesus had a question or two for the disciples: "Why are you afraid? Have you still no faith?" They are, as we would be under such circumstances, understandably speechless; except for their expressed amazement and awe at Jesus' way with the weather.

It strikes me as ironic that the wind and the sea obey Jesus, but that disciples of every time and place are less responsive to Jesus' admonitions, guidance and direction. I believe my failure to trust God's faithfulness and follow Jesus in obedience can be attributed to my lack of faith in God's unconditional love for me. Grasped by the grace and the love of God in Christ, I pray with the psalmist in Psalm 65:6–8: "Clothed in power, you steady the mountains, you still the roaring seas, the restless waves, the raging nations. People everywhere stand amazed at what you do; east and west shout for joy."

Surprises

August 20, 2020

When Jesus was not far from the house, the centurion
sent friends to say to him, "Lord, do not trouble yourself,
for I am not worthy to have you come under my roof;
therefore I did not presume to come to you. But only
speak the word and let my servant be healed . . . " When
Jesus heard this he was amazed at the centurion's words
and turning to the crowed that followed him, Jesus said,
"I tell you, not even in Israel have I found such faith."

(Luke 7:5–7, 9)

JERRY, A LONG-TERM MEMBER OF the Saturday morning men's Bible
study, did not believe that Jesus could be amazed or surprised by
anything. Period. He was adamant and he wasn't alone. Jerry wondered if maybe it was a bad translation. "Jesus is God; he knows
everything; nothing would surprise Jesus," another member of the
Bible study chimed in. We were discussing the story of Jesus healing the Roman centurion's servant in Luke 7 and I was attempting
to offer an alternative interpretation.

"Jesus was human and divine," I said. "That's the mystery of
the incarnation. The Word became flesh and lived among us, as
John 1:14 says." I continued, "Hebrews chapter two says that Jesus

'had to become like his brothers and sisters in every respect, so that he might be a merciful and faithful high priest in the service of God.'" I tried to make the case that in his humanity, Jesus, could be amazed and/or surprised. That's the plain meaning of the text, I argued. But I wasn't making much headway. Most of the men gathered around the table in the church library were convinced they were right and I was wrong. It was a lively standoff.

The gospels of Luke and Mark record two occasions when Jesus was amazed. One is in Luke 7, where Jesus expresses astonishment at the centurion's faith. The other is Mark 6, when Jesus was surprised by people's *lack* of faith. Teaching in his hometown of Nazareth, the locals were "astounded" by Jesus' wisdom and reports of his deeds of power. They knew Jesus the carpenter and knew his family too. Mark reports that his neighbors "took offense at him,"—as in—*Who does Jesus think he is?* Mark also writes that, Jesus "could do no deed of power there except that he laid his hands on a few sick people and cured them. He concludes, "Jesus was amazed at their unbelief."

To be surprised is to feel wonder, astonishment or amazement at something unanticipated. Jesus' surprise at the centurion's faith was a joyful wonder. Jesus' surprise in the face of the unbelief of his Nazarene neighbors was sorrowful. We've had more than our usual share of surprises over the last six months. Some are joyful, but most are sorrowful: over 171,000 deaths from the COVID-19 in the U.S. alone, on top of quarantines, sheltering in place, record unemployment, financial instability, a deeply polarized electorate, a struggling economy, issues of racial injustice, and all kinds of uncertainty about the future.

Six months ago, I didn't see the surprises coming. (Who could? They're surprises!) As I've mentioned before, on February 27th, Ann and I left for a three-week vacation in Texas and Colorado. The surprises started slowly and then escalated faster than we could keep up. I remember the weekend of March 13–15 like it was yesterday: Friday night dinner with friends at a packed San Antonio, Texas restaurant. The next morning we left for Dallas area, to be with our daughter Emily and her family. We stopped for lunch at a fast-food restaurant outside of Waco. The dining room had just closed and the staff was taking orders at a makeshift counter outside the entrance. That was the first of our pandemic surprises. By the middle of the following week, we were in lockdown and life had completely changed. New words like "sheltering in place" and "social distancing" began to pepper our conversations.

Sammamish Hills Lutheran Church has experienced sorrowful surprises. Several members of our congregational family have lost loved ones and have been unable to avail themselves of the traditional rituals of Christian grief, mourning and hope. Pretty much any and every gathering in our church's sanctuary and facilities is now online. Our buildings stand empty. Meetings and activities of all sorts were cancelled

Our congregation has had its share of joyful surprises as well. I've been blessed by your personal stories of caring neighbors and friends sharing their love for others with kind and thoughtful gifts. Church members, friends, the church council, the call committee, and staff have stepped up with servant leadership time and again helping us navigate all manner of pandemic related changes and surprises. They've adapted to life in the pandemic with creativity, resilience and grace. One of the sweetest surprises of the last six months has been the wonderful gift of online worship featuring the weekly offerings of our musicians and their inspiring joyful music.

I want to be attentive to God's surprises. I pray for the capacity to receive each day's surprises, whether they come as joy or sorrow. Like the centurion, I'd like to surprise Jesus now and then. I learned about surprising Jesus in Ron Hansen's novel, *Mariette in Ecstasy.* Mariette wrote a letter to her former Mother Superior at The Sisters of the Crucifixion, an upstate New York convent. Taking the long view after a life of many tests and trials, Mariette wrote:

> We try to be formed and held and kept by Christ but instead he offers us freedom. And now when I try to know his will, his kindness floods me, his great love overwhelms me, and I hear him whisper: "Surprise me." [1]

1. Hansen, *Mariette in Ecstasy,* 179.

Pastors

August 24, 2020

The gifts Christ gave were that some would be apostles, some prophets, some evangelists, some pastors and teachers, to equip the saints for the work of ministry, for building up the body of Christ. (Eph 4:11–12)

My vocation—my call to pastoral ministry—was a modest one. There was no bolt from the blue, no epiphany, no Saul/Paul dropped to his knees by the blinding light of the risen Jesus on the road to Damascus with a call to go and evangelize the world. (See St. Paul's conversion-vocation story in Acts 9). I discerned my call to pastoral ministry in the summer of 1967 while working as a counselor at Camp Metigoshe, a Lutheran camp in the Turtle Mountains of North Dakota. I was twenty years old.

One of our weekend assignments as counselors that summer was to lead Sunday morning worship services in small, rural congregations for vacationing pastors. One Sunday after I'd preached at a worship service at a Lutheran church in Bisbee, North Dakota, an elderly member of the church told me I should be a pastor. No one had ever said anything like that to me before and I took her words to heart. Later that summer I talked with Pastor Mark Ronning, the camp's executive director, about being a pastor. He encouraged me to attend seminary and prepare myself for the Lutheran ministry.

I began my studies at Luther Theological Seminary in St. Paul, Minnesota fifty years ago this month. While in seminary, I studied theology, pastoral care, worship, Greek, preaching and biblical studies—as well as electives like administration and Christian education. After three years of academic work and one year of internship, I was ordained and accepted my first call as the pastor of Shepherd by the Sea Lutheran Church in Malibu, California.

During my internship I began putting into practice what I'd learned at seminary: planning and leading worship, preaching, officiating at weddings, baptizing, leading funerals and burying the dead, pastoral counseling, meeting with the church council, and teaching confirmation. There is only so much one can learn from books; I learned how to be a pastor by doing what pastors *do*. What pastors *do* is outlined in the letter of call of the Evangelical Lutheran Church in America.

My first letter of call was given to me in 1974; my last letter of call was given to me in 1992. I retired in 2014. While there have been minor changes to the wording of the basic letter of call, the substance remains the same. Lutheran pastors are called to preach and teach the Word of God, administer Holy Baptism and Holy Communion, lead worship, proclaim forgiveness, provide pastoral care, speak for justice, encourage people to prepare for the ministry (like the woman in Bisbee, North Dakota did for me), educate people on the work of the ELCA, equip people for witness and service, and guide people in sharing God's love in word and deed. That's what pastors are called and sent to do.

Over the years, I've come to believe that a core expectation of pastors is that we should practice what we preach. In other words, *we* should do what *we* say *you* should do. The last thing congregations need is more hypocrites, especially in the pulpit. I've joked with Ann that I'd like to get a tattoo on the inside of my left wrist that reads: PWIP, as in, *Practice What I Preach*. St. Paul wrote to the Romans that all have sinned and fall short of the glory of God. "All" means all, as in *all people*, *all Christians* and *all pastors*. Like everyone else, pastors are human, sinful, broken, and flawed. What helps is when people and pastors are able to fess up to their sins and forgive each other. At our humble, healthy and loving best, that's usually good enough to maintain the gift of Christian community.

Sammamish Hills Lutheran Church is in an extended season of pastoral transitions. Thankfully, as St. Paul wrote to the Ephesians, the work of the ministry is not solely the responsibility of pastors. In fact, part of the pastor's job, as both St. Paul and the ELCA letter of call describe it, is to, "equip you for witness and service and guide you in proclaiming God's love through word and deed." This church is abundantly blessed with all manner of gifted, skilled and ably equipped people to do the work of ministry and build up the body of Christ.

Still, we need pastors. I'm grateful for the gift of having served these last two years with Pastor Eric Hanson. Working with Pastor Eric has been a joyous and grace-filled privilege. I'm thankful for his pastoral ministry. As he prepares to leave us, I wish him well, and, like you, I will miss him. At the time of this writing, we are awaiting word from Bishop Shelley Bryan Wee about another interim pastor who will join me in serving you during this time of transition.

In the meantime, I have four prayer requests for you. First, pray for God's blessings on Pastor Eric as he begins his new ministry in Minnesota. Second, pray for our new interim pastor. Third, pray for the call committee and their search for a new lead pastor. Finally, remember that your new lead pastor is out there waiting to be called. Pray that God will continue to prepare her or him for the good and godly work of serving Sammamish Hills Lutheran Church.

Foundations

August 27, 2020

Everyone who hears these words of mine and acts on
them will be like a wise man who built his house on
rock. The rain fell, the floods came, and the winds blew
and beat on that house, but it did not fall, because it had
been founded on rock. (Matt 7:24–25)

I'M MINDFUL THAT AS I type these words, hundreds of thousands
of our neighbors in Louisiana and Texas have fled for their lives,
lest they become victims of Hurricane Laura. I pray for safety, shelter, and relief for our fellow citizens.

When I think about the rain, floods, and winds that beat
upon the houses of our lives, I realize that for me, it's not so much
that I'm worried about the troubles ahead or the problems or perils
that may come my way. I am concerned about how I will *respond*.
For me, the question is not, *Will bad things happen?* The question
is, *Am I ready?*

Bad things happen all the time. Even so, we often feel blindsided by the storms of life seldom more so than during the current
pandemic and its collateral impacts. Some days we are spared;
some days we are not. Some days it's just a drizzle; other days it
feels like a flood. We are not invincible; we are vulnerable. Jesus

was a realist and he knew a thing or two about the storms of life. His understanding of our fragile state was summed up in a sobering passage in Matthew's gospel: "God makes the sun rise on the evil and on the good and sends the rain on the righteous and on the unrighteous." (5:45)

When my world is rocked, will I stay the course or be overwhelmed? Will God's grace and the gifts of faith, hope, and love, help me keep my head above water? The question is not how can I be spared or how can I avoid life's pain and suffering. The question is, *upon what foundation am I building the house of my life?*

When troubles come, when the storms of life surge, are we ready? At the end of the Sermon on the Mount after having spelled out what it means to follow Jesus, our Lord invites and challenges us to build the house of our lives on the rock of his words. The *Message* puts it this way: "These words I speak to you are not incidental additions to your life, homeowner improvements to your standard of living. They are foundational words, words to build a life on" (Matt 7:24–25).

St. Paul built the house of his life on the solid rock of Jesus. Writing to the Philippians, he spoke of his new life in Christ: "Whatever gains I had, I have come to regard as loss because of Christ. More than that, I regard everything as loss because of the surpassing value of knowing Christ Jesus my Lord. For his sake I have suffered the loss of all things and I regard them as rubbish in order that I may gain Christ and be found in him (3:7–9b).

So, here's some good news. We are saved by grace through faith. Our redemption, our salvation, is not about whether or not we are ready for the next bad thing. Saving faith is believing God's promises have our names written on them and trusting that God loves us no matter what; no matter what happens and no matter how we do or don't cope with it. What's more, we are not alone. Ever. "God is our refuge and strength, a very present help in trouble. Therefore we will not fear, though the earth should change, though the mountains shake in the heart of the sea; though its waters roar and foam, though the mountains tremble with its tumult (Ps 46:1–3).

Ann and I live in downtown Issaquah. Several years ago homeowners in our neighborhood jacked up their old house and put a new foundation under it. I'm happy to report the house is still standing. So, if you think you've been building the house of your life on sand, if you're not sure you have a firm footing, it's never too late to jack up the house of your life and put a new foundation under it. Jesus, who stilled storm tossed seas, is still calming fearful hearts. Christ is the cornerstone. His word is our firm foundation.

Cornerstone Prayer

September 3, 2020

> Because of this [Jesus' teachings about the Bread of
> Life] many of his disciples turned back and no longer
> went about him. So Jesus asked the twelve, "Do you also
> wish to go away?" Simon Peter answered him, "Lord, to
> whom can we go? You have the words of eternal life."
> (John 6:66–68)

PRETTY MUCH EVERY ONE OF my days starts the same. I get up and
put away the previous night's dishes. I go out and get the newspaper
and give the front page a quick look. I make a cup of coffee. I sit
down with my cup of coffee and do my morning readings and prayer.
Some folks call the formal, liturgical version of my day's beginnings,"
morning- prayer" or "lauds" (typically chanted or said at daybreak).
I call it my cornerstone prayer. Later in the morning, time permit-
ting, there will be other prayers and readings but my cornerstone
prayer is *foundational*. It's the first prayer I pray every day.

My cornerstone prayer begins with several Bible readings:
"Gracious God, I watch for you, my strong tower of safety. I celebrate your strength and rejoice in your love each morning, for you
are my tower of safety, my haven in time of distress" (Ps 59:16).
"For freedom, Christ has set us free. Do not use your freedom as

an opportunity for self-indulgence. Live by the Spirit and do not gratify the desires of the flesh; these prevent you from doing what you want . . . The fruit of the Spirit is love, joy, peace, patience, kindness, generosity, faithfulness, gentleness and self-control. There is no law against such things" (Gal 5:16–17, 22–23). "I can do all things through Christ who strengthens me" (Phil 4:13). "Give your entire attention to what God is doing right now, and don't get worked up about what may or may not happen tomorrow. God will help you deal with whatever hard things come up when the time comes (Matt. 6:34, MSG).

After the readings, I pray short prayers for my family, myself, and the day ahead as well as other brief intercessions. The whole thing takes ten or fifteen minutes tops.

My cornerstone readings and prayers are not spiritual insurance; they will not prevent anything bad from happening to me, or to those I love. They will not protect me from the slings and arrows of the day. My daily practice is not some form of spiritual *quid pro quo*: I do this and God will do that. As I read and pray, I have no idea what will happen between praying these prayers in the morning and turning in for the night some fifteen hours later. I do the readings and pray simple prayers in obedience to the invitation of Jesus: "When you are praying, do not heap up empty phrases as the Gentiles do; for they think that they will be heard because of their many words. Do not be like them, for your Father knows what you need before you ask him" (Matt 6:7–8).

As I set the cornerstone for the day by reading brief passages of Holy Scripture and offering prayers, I do so mindful of two truths. First, I am subject to failing to live what I read and forgetting who I want to be as the Apostle James wrote in his letter: "For if any are hearers of the word and not doers, they are like those who look at themselves in a mirror; they look at themselves and, on going away, immediately forget what they were like" (1:23–24). Second, God is love and will never forsake me or abandon me. As I am with people virtually or in person in the course of my day, I want to remember what I have read and be mindful of God's loving presence.

When Guglielmo Marconi, the father of modern radio, was twenty years old, he created a clunky wireless device in his father's basement that could transmit radio signals. Years later, when the Titanic sank on April 15, 1912, Marconi—by then a Nobel Prize winner—was credited with saving over 700 lives thanks to the ship's modern radio, which made it possible to call in rescue ships at night. According to Dan Zadra and Kobi Yamada in their book, *10: What's On Your Top Ten List?*, Marconi was convinced that sound never dies; that sound waves, once emitted from a radio or the vibrating strings of a Stradivarius violin never die; they get weaker, but live on forever. Marconi figured that we just hadn't built a radio powerful enough to recapture the signals. Near the end of his life, Marconi dreamed of creating a device that would let us tap into these eternal frequencies. He wanted us to be able to hear everything, from Shakespeare giving an actor a line, to Jesus delivering the Sermon on the Mount.[1]

I sit down with my cup of coffee in the darkness of the early morning hours. I do so trusting the promise of Isa 55:10–11: "For as the rain and the snow come down from heaven and do not return there until they have watered the earth, making it bring forth and sprout, giving seed to the sower and bread to the eater, so shall my word be that goes out of my mouth; it shall not return to me empty, but it shall accomplish that which I purpose, and succeed in the thing for which I sent it." I savor the living Word of God, listening for the "eternal frequencies" of sacred texts that are thousands of years old, speaking new life into my anxious and hopeful heart. Readings read and prayers prayed; I'm ready for a new day.

---

1. Zadra and Yamada, *10: What's On Your Top Ten List?*

Simple Pleasures

September 11, 2020

O Lord, how manifold are your works! In wisdom you
have made them all; the earth is full of your creatures.
Yonder is the sea, great and wide, creeping things
innumerable are there, living things both small and
great. There go the ships, and Leviathan that you formed
to sport in it. (Ps 104:26)

"WHAT ARE YOU DOING?" the waitress asks the diner. "Oh, I'm
making a list of my favorite words," he says. She says, "My favorite
word is 'soap,'" she says sitting down next to the diner. She playfully
enunciates "soap" by drawing out the P and popping her cheeks.
She goes on to repeat her favorite word, "soap," again and again,
each time drawing out the P and popping her cheeks with growing
exuberance. The diner soon joins in as they fill the mostly empty
café with a rousing chorus of the word "soap." "Aye," she sighs,
"simple pleasures." The scene is from the 2018 film, *Sometimes,
Always, Never,* a sad quirky wonder of a story about a father looking for his lost son with multiple references to the parable of the
prodigal son and the game of Scrabble. [1]

---

1. Hunter, Carl, director. 2018. *Sometimes, Always, Never.* Blue Fox
Entertainment.

I cannot deny or ignore the pain, uncertainty, and suffering that seems to engulf us, and our neighbors, on a daily basis. We are living through a pandemic, a faltering economy, record unemployment, racial strife, a polarized electorate, and wildfires in Washington, Oregon, and California. What's more, today is the nineteenth commemoration of the 9/11 attacks on the Twin Towers, the Pentagon, and the crash of United Airlines Flight 93 in Pennsylvania. Sometimes it feels like it's way too much.

In the darkness, there are slivers of light. Like a firefly softly illuminating the night, the "simple pleasures" are undeserved blessings that come to us when we least expect them. I don't have to be on the prowl for simple pleasures; they just show up and present themselves to me. Sitting at my desk one recent afternoon I saw a big cat crossing the backyard; it took me a moment to realize it was a big cat all right – it was a bobcat. It's a Sunday afternoon. I'm sitting at the picnic table by the creek (we live in downtown Issaquah on the East Fork of the Issaquah Creek). I look up and there they are: a raccoon family of four slowly making their way up the eastside of the creek one after another. I've never seen a bobcat in the back yard or four raccoons making their way up the creek. The psalmist writing in Psalm 104 got it right: God made the Leviathan for the sport of it, for the fun of it. If we have eyes to see and ears to hear, we get a front row seat at God's wonder theater and life's simple, grace-filled pleasures.

In the eighth chapter of his letter to the church at Rome, St. Paul writes, "Likewise the Spirit helps us in our weakness; for we do not know how to pray as we ought, but that very Spirit intercedes for us with sighs too deep for words" 8:26). For years I always thought that what Paul is writing about is my inability to articulate my pain, to put it into words. Since I can't, the Spirit does it for me.

My understanding of this passage changed one afternoon at Huntington Beach in Southern California. It was late in the day and I was sitting by myself drinking in the view. The first thing that happened was that I saw a pod of dolphins leaping and diving in unison just past where the waves were breaking. It was thrilling. Next up, two women slowly walking down the beach. They were wearing long dresses that reminded me of Amish or Mennonite women I have seen in Lancaster County, Pennsylvania. Later, when I saw them coming back up the beach, they were carrying their shoes and walking in the wet sand. Seeing the dolphins swimming and the women walking triggered a feeling of joy I couldn't put into words. That's when my understanding of Romans 8:26 changed as I wondered to myself, *Maybe, sometimes, what is in fact actually too deep for words, is praise, joy, and life's simple pleasures.*

A 2020 Voter's Guide

September 17, 2020

> The first thing I want you to do is pray. Pray every way
> you know how, for everyone you know. Pray especially
> for rulers and their governments to rule well so we can
> be quietly about our business of living simply, in humble
> contemplation. This is the way our Savior God wants us
> to live. (1 Tim 2:1–2, *The Message*)

MY FATHER COULDN'T BELIEVE HIS ears. He was angry and gave
me an earful. During the Sunday morning worship service, our
pastor had introduced a member of the church who was running
for congress during the announcements. It just so happened that
the man was a member of a different political party than that of
my father. (I would like to think that he would have been just as
upset if the candidate was a member of his own preferred party).
I don't remember if my father complained to our pastor or not.
What I do remember is that the candidate won his election and
served several terms in the House of Representatives. I doubt that
the pastor's endorsement contributed to the congressman's election, but who knows?

Some years later, I was serving as an associate pastor in San
Diego. A campaign staffer for a man who was running for local

office called the church and wanted to know if the candidate could address the congregation on Sunday morning. The senior pastor and I discussed our options, none of which seemed viable. At the time, our practice was to introduce visitors during the Sunday morning announcements, and so we agreed that if the candidate attended worship, we would introduce him just like any other first-time visitor. Sure enough, the candidate showed up, but rather than take a seat in a pew, he stood just inside the door to the sanctuary. We introduced him together with other visitors but without making any reference to his candidacy. He wanted to use the church for partisan purposes but we resisted. I have no regrets. I believe we did the right thing.

As you may know, pastors of both conservative and progressive churches take sides and endorse candidates for public office. Sometimes religious groups publish voter's guides identifying which candidates or propositions parishioners should vote for. That has never been my practice and I have no intention of starting now. Don't get me wrong. I belong to a political party and I'm going to vote on November 3. What's more, just like you, I hope the candidates I cast my ballot for get elected. However, I don't believe it is my place to advocate for a particular party, candidate or proposition. So I won't. (By the way, if you have any family or friends who live in Santa Barbara, California, would you please tell them to vote for our nephew's wife who's running for the local school board? Just kidding).

In 1929, my grandmother, Bernice Thomas, was elected to the Grover, Colorado City Council. Nine years after women got the vote, my grandmother was a member of the town's first all-women's city council. According to the Grover entry on the Weld County History website:

> Mayor Elizabeth Lower and several of her "feminine cohorts" were fed up with the antics of a pool hall proprietor who condoned bootlegging and gambling, a prospect which, to the women of the day, presented a serious safety issue to the community, and especially to the children of the area. This unique town board also

significantly reduced the civic debt of the town, which to that point, no male board could accomplish.

My grandmother was a Christian who wanted to make Grover, Colorado a better place to live. Committed to the common good, she ran for public office and was elected to serve her community.

Neither Sammamish Hills Lutheran Church nor I will be publishing a voter's guide for the 2020 election, but I would like to offer you some guidance just the same. First, don't let the headlines distract you from the task at hand: thoughtfully and prayerfully considering voting for candidates and propositions that reflect your core values and convictions.

Second, Holy Scripture provides the criteria for what matters most: loving our neighbors as ourselves. When asked which law was the greatest, Jesus was unequivocal: "You shall love the Lord your God with all your heart, and with all your soul, and with all your mind. This is the greatest and first commandment. And a second it like it: You shall love your neighbor as yourself. On these two hang all the law and the prophets" (Matt 22:37–40). As you prepare your ballot, consider how your vote will impact the lives of your neighbors, near and far. Is my vote an act of loving my neighbor as I love myself? Will my vote help or hurt my neighbor? Will my vote increase or diminish the quality of life for my neighbor?

Third, remember, your vote counts. Rowan Hinds, a former mayor of my town of Issaquah, won his second election by the thinnest of margins; according to Mr. Hinds, he won by twelve or thirteen votes. The outcome of that election was a civic reality check for me: My vote and your vote make a difference. So, vote! Remember to mail in your ballot (no stamp is required for mail-in, but it must be postmarked by Election Day) or place your ballot in a ballot drop box by 8:00 p.m. on Election Day. Plan ahead so as to avoid lines.

Fourth, join me in praying: A Prayer For Responsible Citizenship from *Evangelical Lutheran Worship*:

> Lord God, you call your people to honor those in authority. Help us elect trustworthy leaders, participate in wise decisions for our common life, and serve our neighbors

in local communities. Bless the leaders of our land, that we may be at peace among ourselves and be a blessing to other nations of the earth, through Jesus Christ, our Savior and Lord. Amen.[1]

1. *Evangelical Lutheran Worship*, 77.

The Righteous Are Not Afraid of Evil Tidings

September 24, 2020

They [the righteous] are not afraid of evil tidings;
their hearts are firm, secure in the Lord. (Ps 112:7)

THE FIRST TIME I READ this verse it stopped me dead in my tracks. *Wait just a minute,* I thought to myself, *More often than not, evil tidings*—also known as bad news—*pretty much knocks me for a loop; it sours my mood and rocks my world. Who are these righteous people who are fearless in the face of bad news? I sure would like to meet them!*

Exactly how righteous does one have to be in order to be fearless in the face of evil tidings and bad news? What kind of spiritual fortitude is required to dropkick bad news and send it packing? As I thought about it, it slowly dawned on me: What is variously translated as "the righteous," and "the strong of heart" is describing people just like you and me, who are anchored *in* and tethered *to* the promises of God. They are people who trust God and trust God's promises. Moreover, the righteous and strong-hearted among us are blessed with a spiritual capacity to maintain the trust that God will not forsake them; that God is with them no matter what.

As is always the case with Holy Scripture, context is helpful. The heading for Psalm 112 in the *New Revised Standard Version* is, "Blessings of the Righteous." The heading summarizes the psalm/prayer. It affirms that those who fear the Lord are, "happy and greatly delight in the Lord's commandments." Their wealth is a testimony to their righteousness (their riches are not self-serving). "They are gracious and merciful. It is well with those who deal generously and lend, who conduct their affairs with justice. For the righteous will never be moved . . . They have distributed freely, they have given to the poor; their righteousness endures forever." These are the people who are fearless in the face of bad news.

Psalm 112 is a prayer of praise to God and a celebration of people who are upright, righteous and pious. It's a prayer of gratitude for people for whom the *good news* of God's love almost always eclipses the *bad news*, no matter what the bad news *is*. Don't get me wrong—bad news is bad news. It can knock us for a loop and rock our world. A loved one dies suddenly; a friend or family member is diagnosed with cancer; a coworker is unexpectedly laid off; a father, mother, son or daughter is diagnosed with COVID-19 and hospitalized. Let me repeat: bad news is bad news. What Psalm 112 teaches me is that it is possible, in the face of bad news, to be mindful of—and strengthened by—God's love and faithfulness.

I don't want to minimize the pain, suffering, loss and the grief that accompanies unexpected bad news. Nor do I want to encourage a thoughtless, superficial piety that glosses over pain and loss. I wouldn't think of quoting this verse to anyone who was hurting, mourning or reeling in the face of loss. Psalm 112 is a profile of what life looks like when someone delights in God's will and ways and is able to endure hardship. In his commentary on Psalm 112, John Goldingay writes:

> People living the good life do not fear for themselves; their reliance on God means they do not fear trouble coming. When it threatens, they know God will deliver them . . . Such promises are risky and do not always

correspond to experience, but that is no reason for denying them their place in Holy Scripture. [1]

These days the bad news is relentless. Texts, tweets, social media posts, print media, radio and television broadcasts are filled with local, national, and global bad news. Managing one's news stream requires wisdom and vigilance. At times, it feels like I'm drinking from a fire hose; I can't take it all in. I want to be informed but I don't want to be overwhelmed. So, I do my best to stay abreast of current events, and to take a break from non-stop news so as to get perspective on what matters most—distinguishing what I'm powerless to do anything about from where I can make a difference.

Every morning I read the following quote from St. Francis de Sales. (I shared it with you in a previous letter). This wisdom helps me trust God's love and faithfulness in the face of bad news:

> I recommend to you holy simplicity. Look straight in front of you and not at those dangers you see in the distance. As you say, to you they look like armies, but they are only willow branches; and while you are looking at them you may take a false step. Let us be firmly resolved to serve God with our whole heart and life. Beyond that, let us have no care about tomorrow. Let us think only of living today well, and when tomorrow comes, it also will be today and we can think about it then. [2]

1. Goldingay, *Psalms, Volume 3*, 314.
2. DeSales and De Chantal, *Letters of Spiritual Direction*, 98–99.

Nothing Can Separate Us from the Love of God

October 1, 2020

> In all these things we are more than conquerors through Christ who loved us. For I am convinced that neither death, nor life, nor angels, nor rulers, nor things present, nor things to come, nor powers, nor height, nor depth, nor anything else in all creation, will be able to separate us from the love of God in Christ Jesus our Lord.
>
> (Rom 8:37–39)

I WAS VISITING WITH PR. Ron Marshall on Zoom. We were both students at Luther Theological Seminary in the early 1970s and we were discussing memorable chapel sermons. We acknowledged that we didn't remember many of the chapel sermons we heard; in my case I remembered two or three over the course of attending chapel for three years. As we spoke with each other we found ourselves talking about Dr. Paul Sponheim, a professor of systematic theology at Luther. To our mutual amazement, we both remembered the chapel sermon Dr. Sponheim preached on Romans 8:35–39.

St. Paul begins the passage with a fearless and penetrating question: "Who will separate us from the love of Christ? Will hardship or distress, or persecution, or famine, or nakedness, or peril, or sword?" What was memorable about Dr. Sponheim's sermon on this text was what happened *after* he read the passage: he offered a litany of things that felt like or seemed to be things what *could* separate us from the love of God in Christ Jesus.

I'd never ever heard anyone take a text and update it in such a powerful way. I don't remember the details of Dr. Sponheim's list, but here's mine: *Who will separate us from the love of Christ? A pandemic? Sheltering in place? Social distancing? Quarantines? A divided and conflicted electorate? Record unemployment? Racism? White supremacy? Fires? Hurricanes? Tornadoes? Floods?* No! Nothing can separate us from the love of God in Christ Jesus our Lord.

For as long as I can remember, the promise that nothing, no one, no situation, or circumstance, no hardship or distress, no trouble or peril. can separate us from the love of Christ has been an anchor to which I tether my storm-tossed anxious heart to. Even when I'm *feeling* like I'm at the end of my emotional rope, or down for the count, I believe—Lord, help my unbelief— in the gospel truth of St. Paul's reassuring words.

Sheltering in place and stuck inside our home due to unhealthy air quality from regional fires, I am tempted to another bout of self-pity. Once I've identified what's going on, I am, thankfully, quick to realize that my current grievances are nothing compared to what people who are truly suffering are living with.

In his commentary on this passage from Romans 8, N.T. Wright suggests that the whole of Romans chapters 5–8 has been about *assurance.*

> When we understand [that we are saved by grace through faith] that's assurance . . . John Donne, likened the love of God to a circle, seeing that it is endless. It rules victoriously over death and life alike, over powers in heaven and on earth. And since it is love's nature to bind the beloved to itself, Paul is convinced that 'nothing in all creation can separate us from the love of God in Christ Jesus our

Lord . . . The end of Romans 8 deserves to be written in letters of fire on the living tablets of our hearts. [1]

That's the promise, no matter what. Period.

1. Wright, *Paul For Everyone, Romans Part 1*, 159, 161.

Savor the Wonder

Thursday, October 8, 2020

Look at the birds of the air; they neither sow nor reap
nor gather into barns, and yet your heavenly Father
feeds them. (Matt 6:26)

I WAS SURPRISED THAT SEPTEMBER 22nd was the first day of autumn. I was wondering if the first day of autumn was September 20th or the 21 and so I had to look it up. I'm aware of the season's rhythms but I am not a naturalist. I can identify a 1934 Ford or a 1952 Chevrolet but I couldn't identify a warbler or a wren if my life depended on it. On our morning walks, Ann is always the first one to notice the changing colors; the glimmering gold and robust red of green trees giving way to the kaleidoscope that is creation's annual, autumnal, light show. I'm slow to notice, but grateful for the beauty.

Returning from our morning walks, we've started walking out to the creek to look for salmon. I haven't seen any salmon yet, but Ann saw one the other day. Our small plot of God's good earth is alive with moles digging up dirt and squirrels grazing for grub. Last week a bear ambled through and left a gift in our yard. One morning I walked out back to check on the creek; I watched in rapt silence as a Great Blue Heron slowly took flight looking like a small aircraft taking off from a jungle airfield.

In his book, *Christ Plays in Ten Thousand Places*, Eugene Peterson writes:

> Two friends enter a forest. One sees a mass of trees, the other sees spruce and oak and pine and elm. One looks at the ground and sees tangles of needles and brush, the other looks down and sees bloodroot and hepatica and arnica. One looks up and sees a blur of motion through the leaves, the other looks up and sees a Red-Eyed Vireo and a McGillivray Warbler and the Least Flycatcher. Which of the two is more alive to the garden and more in relation to the life that is spilling out and reverberating all through it in colors and songs, forms and movements—and to the God who planted the garden and put us in it? [1]

I confess I am the one who sees the mass of trees, the tangles of needles and the brush and the blur of motion – although I do know a Great Blue Heron when I see one. I am content to enjoy the beauty that surrounds us, even if I can't call it by name. I take delight in the company of those who see spruce and oak and Red-Eyed Vireo, a McGillivray Warbler and a Least Flycatcher. Jesus taught that I could learn a thing or two from the birds of the air and the lilies of the field. He figured remembering that God provides food for the birds of the air and dresses the lilies of the field in couture that would put the stars of Paris Fashion Week to shame, would help center us in God's faithful provision for our needs and the needs of our neighbors. I try to take him at his word.

These days, it feels like the list of things I can worry about is growing. I've got my list; I expect you have yours. In spite of all the temptations to fear and worry, Jesus invites me to drink in the view and savor the wonder of flower and fauna, bird and bear, mole and squirrel, remembering that God has got our backs and that God has got us covered. And that's not all: God is with us and God will not forsake us. Jesus teaches that worry, fear and anxiety will not

1. Peterson, *Christ Plays in Ten Thousand Places*, 80.

change or alter anything. Jesus' admonition in Matthew 6— "Don't worry about your life"—and his redemptive reality check that worrying won't add a single hour to our span of life, frees me to trust that God holds us in the palm of God's hand.

In recent conversations, I've been encouraged by people who are fortified for living in faith, hope, and love by the simple act of being attentive to all the ways that God showers blessings upon us, especially in creation. I am grateful for the wisdom of the poet/ farmer Wendell Berry's, "The Peace of Wild Things." It is a timely word and a soothing balm.

The Peace of Wild Things

When despair for the world grows in me
and I wake in the night at the least sound
in fear of what my life and my children's lives may be,
I go and lie down where the wood drake
rests in his beauty on the water, and the green heron feeds.
I come into the peace of wild things
who do not tax their lives with forethought
of grief. I come into the presence of still water.
And I feel above me the day-blind stars
waiting with their light. For a time
I rest in the grace of the world, and am free. [2]

---

2. Berry, *New Collected Poems*, 129.

Blessed Are The Peacemakers
Thursday, October 15, 2020

Blessed are the peacemakers, for they will be called
children of God. (Matt 5:9)

I WAS SITTING AT MY desk in my office at the church I served in Los
Angeles when I noticed the framed copy of the Beatitudes on the
wall behind me. "Blessed are the peacemakers," caught my eye and
got me thinking about Rey. Rey and Janice, and their sons, Bud and
Jon, were our next-door neighbors. Now and then our children
played with each other, but other than an occasional greeting or a
brief conversation, Rey and I didn't know each other much at all.

Then one day, I broke up a front yard skirmish between one
of our sons and one of Rey and Janice's sons. Apparently, Jon reported to his father Rey that I had grabbed him during the scuffle.
This did not go down so well with neighbor Rey. Did I mention
that Rey was a judo instructor and a Vietnam veteran who had
served in the Special Forces? In any case, in spite of only occasional conversations we were no longer on speaking terms and I
wasn't feeling too good about it.

Sitting in my office, mulling over the "blessed are the peacemakers" beatitude, I had an idea. I typed out a letter, placed it in an
envelope and hand addressed it to Rey. After work, I walked over
to Rey's house, knocked on the door and handed the letter to Bud,

Rey's oldest son. The letter was my attempt to be a peacemaker. In my letter, I explained what happened and I apologized. A few days later, Rey was working in his front yard when I got home from work. Rey said to me, "I got your letter." I replied, "Good; wanna talk?" Rey said yes.

Rey invited me into his house. We sat down at the kitchen table and mended fences. What began as a low-level, next-door-neighbor relationship grew into a new friendship. Rey and Janice started worshiping at the church where I was the pastor. When Janice was diagnosed with cancer, our family and the congregation were able to provide ministries of care and support. The reconciliation of a broken relationship and the fruit of our peacemaking led to countless, mutual acts of love.

Jesus prioritizes reconciling relationships. Matthew chapter five begins with the Beatitudes, including "blessed are the peacemakers." (This is the first of three chapters devoted to Jesus' "Sermon on the Mount.") After informing his followers that they are the "salt of the earth" and the "light of the world," Jesus contrasts various commandments with his own rigorous reinterpretation.

Beginning with the sixth commandment, Jesus says: "You have heard that it was said to those of ancient times, 'You shall not murder; and whoever murders shall be liable to judgment.' But I say to you that if you are angry with a brother or sister, you will be liable to judgment; and if you insult a brother or sister, you will be liable to the council; and if you say, 'You fool,' you will be liable to the hell of fire" (Matt 5:21–22). That's pretty strong stuff! The pinnacle of Jesus' take no prisoners approach to loving relationships in Matthew 5 is his teaching to love our enemies and pray for those who persecute us.

In between reinterpreting the "do not murder" commandment and the teaching to love our enemies and pray for those who persecute us, Jesus provides his beloved with guidance on how to reconcile estranged relationships: "So when you are offering your gift at the altar, if you remember that your brother or sister has something against you, leave your gift there before the altar and go; first be reconciled to your brother or sister and then come and offer your gift" (Matt 5:23–24). In other words, as far as Jesus is concerned, repairing estranged relationships takes precedence over my worship offering.

Earlier this week I was sitting at my desk making an online offering to the church. According to Jesus, had I thought of someone that I had hurt or someone who had something against me, I should have stopped making my donation, reached out to the person I had hurt, done whatever I could to heal the hurt and restore the relationship, and *then* resumed making the online donation.

With an election less than three weeks away and political polarizations proliferating, the call to peacemaking and loving my enemies is a bracing, counter-cultural invitation to action. At times like these, being called and sent to be the salt of the earth and the light of the world feels like a pretty tall order. And yet, it is the way of Christ; it is how we, the beloved of God, take up our crosses and follow Jesus.

Jesus put loving our neighbors as ourselves right up there with loving God with all our hearts, all our souls and with all our minds. (Matt 22:36–40). In his first letter to the Christians at Corinth, St. Paul profiles what peacemaking love looks like: "Love is patient; love is kind; love is not envious or boastful or arrogant or rude. It does not insist on its own way; it is not irritable or resentful; it does not rejoice in wrongdoing, but rejoices in the truth. It bears all things, believes all things, hopes all things, endures all things. Love never ends" (1 Cor 13:4–8a).

Returning home from church one Sunday, President Abraham Lincoln was asked by a companion how he liked the sermon. Mr. Lincoln responded that he thought the message was well prepared and thoughtfully constructed, but it lacked the most important ingredient. His companion asked what that was. The president responded: "The preacher failed to ask us to do anything great." I want to ask you to do something great: Spirit-led and Spirit-empowered, put the great commandments into practice: love God with all your heart, soul, and mind—and love your neighbor as yourself.

Perfect Imperfection

October 22, 2020

If you wish to be perfect, go, sell your possessions, and give the money to the poor, and you will have treasure in heaven; then come and follow me. (Matt 19:21)

MY FATHER WAS A PERFECTIONIST. Everything had to be just right. The problem was, nothing ever was—perfect, that is. After moving into the new family home in Pacoima, California, my father decided that he wanted to plant a warm-climate perennial ground cover called Dichondra in the front yard. He worked tirelessly caring for the lawn. It was as close to perfection as anything I've ever seen. I learned to mow a lawn on Dichondra grass and it was a weekly challenge to get it just right. I usually fell short of the mark. Years later we were talking about his perfectionism and I asked my father for his definition. His answer was sobering: "Perfection means nothing is ever good enough."

In her book, *Amazing Grace: A Vocabulary of Faith,* Kathleen Norris writes: "Perfectionism is one of the scariest words I know." Ms. Norris believes that perfectionism is "a serious psychological affliction that makes people too timid to take necessary risks and causes them to suffer when, although they've done the best they can, their efforts fall short of some imaginary, and usually unattainable standard." [1]

The good news about the word "perfect" according to Ms. Norris, is that as used in the New Testament it is "not a scary word, so much as a scary translation. The word that has been translated as 'perfect' does not mean to set forth an impossible goal, or the perfectionism that would have me strive for it at any cost. It is taken from a Latin word meaning complete, entire; full-grown. To those who originally heard it, the word would convey 'mature' rather than what we mean today by 'perfect.'" [2]

I do my best with whatever task is at hand. I want to get things right. More often than not, I'm content with good enough. At times, I go for the gold and strive for excellence. But not perfection. It's simply too tall an order. I've been reading Peter Guralnick's book, *Sam Phillips: The Man Who Invented Rock 'n' Roll*. Mr. Phillips, the founder of Sun Records in Memphis, Tennessee, discovered Howlin' Wolf, Ike Turner, Jerry Lee Lewis, Johnny Cash and Elvis Presley.

According to Mr. Guralnick, Sam Phillips loved "perfect imperfection." Citing his earliest recordings (including "Rocket 88," which many rock historians consider the very first rock 'n' roll record), Mr. Phillips believed that, "the inspired accident was what you were always looking for, so long as it didn't drown out what you were trying to get across." [3]

Our lives in Christ are a work in progress. None of us will ever approach anything close to perfection. Maybe the most we can hope for—in ourselves and in others—is the spiritual equivalent of "perfect imperfection." At our best we love because God first loved us (1 John 4:19). We believe, in spite of our unbelief (Mark 9:24). We hope against hope (Rom 4:18). Like the rich young ruler, were Jesus to invite me to sell everything and give it all to the poor in order to follow him, I expect I too would "walk away grieving," as I also have many possessions" (Matt 19:22). Saved by grace, thanks

---

1. Norris, *Amazing Grace*, 55.
2. Norris, *Amazing Grace*, 55–56.
3. Guralnick, *Sam Phillips*, 606.

to the love of God in Christ, we are free from the burden of perfectionism. "For by a single offering, he [Jesus] has perfected for all time those who are sanctified" (Heb 10:14). In other words, the self-offering of Jesus on the cross has "perfected" us.

I'm encouraged by the wisdom of Kathleen Norris: "Perfection in a Christian sense, means becoming mature enough to give ourselves to others," she writes. "Whatever we have, no matter how little it seems, is something that can be shared with those who are poorer. This sort of perfection demands that we become fully ourselves, as God would have us be: mature, ripe, full, ready for what befalls us, for whatever is to come."[4]

I love Thomas Merton's prayer, "My Lord God, I have no idea where I am going." For me it perfectly sums up the wonder of lovingly following Jesus imperfectly.

> My Lord God,
> I have no idea where I am going.
> I do not see the road ahead of me.
> I cannot know for certain where it will end,
> nor do I really know myself,
> and the fact that I think I am following your will
> does not mean that I am actually doing so.
> But I believe that the desire to please you
> does in fact please you.
> And I hope I have that desire in all that I am doing.
> I hope that I will never do anything apart from that desire.
> And I know that if I do this you will lead me by the right road,
> though I may know nothing about it.
> Therefore will I trust you always though
> I may seem to be lost and in the shadow of death.
> I will not fear, for you are ever with me,
> and you will never leave me to face my perils alone. [5]

---

4 Norris, *Amazing Grace*, 57.

5. Merton, *Thoughts in Solitude*, 79.

With Malice Towards None

November 5, 2020

If anyone is in Christ, there is a new creation; everything
old has passed away; see everything has become new! All
this is from God, who reconciled us to himself through
Christ, and has given us the ministry of reconciliation;
that is, in Christ God was reconciling the world to
himself, not counting their trespasses against them,
and entrusting the message of reconciliation to us. So
we are ambassadors for Christ, since God is making his
appeal through us; we entreat you on behalf of Christ,
be reconciled to God. (2 Cor 5:17–20)

Once a month the transition/interim pastors of the
Northwest Washington Synod of the Evangelical Lutheran Church
meet together for a couple of hours. We check in and discuss the
book we're reading; currently it's *Embracing God's Future Without
Forgetting the Past: A Conversation About Loss, Grief, and Nostalgia
in Congregational Life,* by Michael K. Girlinghouse. We spend
some time "dwelling in the word," using the same passage each
month: 2 Cor 5:16–21. We listen contemplatively as two different
readers read the passage followed by two brief periods of silence.
In the silence, we listen for a word or phrase that captures our

imagination or speaks to us in a timely way. Then we move into Zoom breakout rooms to discuss our word or phrase with one or two other pastors.

This past Monday, the word or phrase that spoke to me in an especially timely manner was "ambassadors of reconciliation." It was the day before the election and I was mindful of the uncertainty many people were feeling about the aftermath of the vote—regardless of the outcome. When I heard the passage read a second time, I realized that the phrase was actually "ambassadors for Christ." I was momentarily caught off guard until I realized that in fact, the work of ambassadors for Christ *is* the ministry of reconciliation. That's St. Paul's point: reconciled to Christ, God has entrusted us with the ministry of reconciliation, reaching out to others through us.

Ambassadors. I serve on a non-profit board with Kathryn Proffitt, former U.S. Ambassador to Malta. A Republican, she served under President Bill Clinton, a Democrat, from 1997–2001. I emailed Ambassador Proffitt and told her I wanted to write something about being ambassadors for Christ and figured I could learn a thing or two from her about the work of an ambassador. Turns out I did. According to Ms. Proffitt, an ambassador "is the highest-ranking person who represents his or her own government while living in another country."

In a letter she received from President Bill Clinton, he wrote, "Always keep in mind that for the government and the people of the Republic of Malta, you and your mission symbolize the United States of America and its values." Ms. Proffitt, a Seventh Day Adventist, sees parallels between her service as an ambassador and being an ambassador for Christ. She writes that Christians, "are not the personal representative of an earthly president or monarch. Rather you are the personal representative of the King of kings, the Lord of lords and the Creator and Ruler of the Universe."[1] Powerful stuff.

Reconciled to God in Christ, we are commissioned in baptism to be ambassadors for Christ, and entrusted with the ministry of reconciliation. We are called, empowered and sent to be

1. Kathryn Proffitt, *Personal Correspondence.*

personal representatives of the Prince of Peace. Jesus said, "Blessed are the peacemakers, for they will be called children of God" (Matt 5:9). Peacemaking, bridge building and the ministry of reconciliation are life-giving and life-saving practices. Broken and estranged relationships are healed and restored, folks who are on the outs with each other are reconciled, and the gift of mutual forgiveness creates fresh starts and new beginnings.

A couple of weeks ago, a friend told me about the "With Malice Toward None Pledge," an initiative of Braver Angels, a citizens' organization of red, blue, and other Americans working for less rancor and more goodwill in our politics. Earlier this week, I checked out the website and signed the pledge which reads:

> Regardless of how the election turns out, I will not hold hate, disdain, or ridicule for those who voted differently from me. Whether I am pleased or upset about the outcome, I will seek to understand the concerns and aspirations of those who voted differently and will look for opportunities to work with people with whom I don't agree. [2]

I'm writing to you on Wednesday evening. The country is still waiting to learn who will be inaugurated as our next president on January 20, 2021. Regardless of who wins the election, we are a polarized and divided people. As an ambassador for Christ, called to be his personal representative, I want to take the ministry of reconciliation seriously—right here, right now.

---

2. Braver Angels website, *The With Malice Toward None Pledge.*

Sit in Your Cell as in Paradise

November 13, 2020

Jesus said: "Whenever you pray, do not be like the hypocrites; for they love to stand and pray in the synagogues and at the street corners, so that they may be seen by others. Truly I tell you, they have received their reward. But whenever you pray, go into your room and shut the door and pray to your Father who is in secret; and your Father who sees in secret will reward you." (Matt 6:5–6)

LAST SUNDAY AFTERNOON I ATTENDED a Zoom conference with Father Luke Dysinger, a Roman Catholic priest and a Benedictine monk of St. Andrew's Abbey, in Valyermo, California. The theme of Father Luke's presentation was "Solitude and Community in a Time of COVID-19." One of Fr. Luke's points was that while the Coronavirus pandemic prevents us from ordinary gatherings, it creates opportunities for small communities and for nurturing times of solitude and contemplation. Referring to the Rule of St. Romuald, Fr. Luke invited us to think of our prayer closet, room, or quiet place as "paradise," as a place to wait on the grace of God. (Monks refer to their personal rooms as "cells.")

Like many of you, I am subject to sheltering-in-place fatigue. Most days, I manage just fine. Some days, I want to break out, hit the road and spend time with family and friends. But I don't. Instead, I give them a call, send an email, or schedule a Zoom get together. I know that for the foreseeable future, I need to continue to do all the things that public health professionals tell me to do: shelter-in-place, social distance, wear a mask and wash my hands. The sobering news that on Thursday, the U.S. set records for with 152,391 cases and 66,606 people hospitalized underscores the need for us to recommit to these simple, life-saving practices. Like it or not, I simply need to stay put and stay home, for my neighbor's sake and for my own.

Which brings me to Fr. Luke and the "Brief Rule of St. Romuald," an eleventh century text that guides the life of monks of the Calmaldolese order of Benedictines. The "Brief Rule," is approximately one hundred words (compared to *the Rule of Saint Benedict* which is ninety-six pages long). Like all Benedictines, St. Romuald was committed to praying the Book of Psalms—all 150 of them. St. Romuald writes:

> Sit in your cell as in paradise . . . The path you must follow is in the Psalms—don't leave it . . . Take every chance you can find to sing the Psalms in your heart and to understand them in your head . . . Above all realize that you are in God's presence, like a little chick tasting and eating nothing but what its mother brings. [1]

On my first sabbatical, I did a private retreat at the New Camaldoli Hermitage in Big Sur, California. All the guests stayed in small trailers or cottages. Our meals were brought to our rooms; we ate alone. Other than singing the Psalms together in the chapel four times a day and attending daily Mass, we did not engage with each other. My room (or cell), together with the sublime beauty of the mountains and coastline of Big Sur, was indeed like a paradise. Over the course of my (mostly silent) retreat, I walked and prayed, read and rested, and wrote in my journal. While eating breakfast

---

1. Contemplation.com, *The Brief Rule of St. Romuald.*

one morning, I spied a red fox outside the sliding glass door of my room. Early one evening, as I watched the sun set on the horizon, I started counting stars. I soon abandoned my counting-the-stars project, lost in the wonder of the dazzling, star-studded night sky.

My time with the monks of New Camaldoli reinforced my belief that I can do all things through Christ who strengthens me, even practicing silence and solitude. (As an extroverted people person, silence and solitude don't come naturally to me, but I'm learning.) My experiences of monastic retreats, together with my personal devotional practices, have been good training for sheltering in place and social distancing. Day by day, I'm learning to see our house, our home, as paradise—a shelter from the storm of the pandemic. Not everyone is as privileged as we are, so I do my best to be grateful.

Making time for solitude, silence, prayer, Bible reading and other devotional practices is a daily lifeline to God. Engaging in these ancient practices helps me lay a solid foundation for the living of my days. St. Romuald believed that sitting and waiting for the daily manna of God's word was paradise.

When we moved into our Issaquah home, we had some friends over for a house blessing. (The technical term is "A Blessing of a Dwelling.") A pastor friend led us in procession through the house one room at a time. We took turns sharing a Bible reading and then praying the appropriate prayer for each room. As we concluded the house blessing, our procession returned to the living room. We gathered around a candle and prayed a prayer of blessing for our home and family.

Re-imagining our home, apartment, room, a favorite chair, or quiet place as holy ground—a paradise where we encounter God—is a life-giving way to experience God's peace and make our way through the pandemic.

Dr. Francis Collins and Psalm 46

November 19, 2020

God is our refuge and strength, a very present help in trouble. Therefore we will not fear, though the earth should change, though the mountains shake in the heart of the sea; though its waters roar and foam, though the mountains tremble with its tumult. (Ps 46:1–3)

I KEEP CHECKING MY CALENDAR. It's November 19, 2020, but with surging COVID-19 cases hospitalizations and deaths, it feels like March or April all over again. With this week's reinstated lock-downs, I'm working hard to remember my frame of mind from last spring: essential travel, no in-person get-togethers, and shelter in place. Yesterday morning, our daughter Rebecca texted our family and proposed a Zoom family Thanksgiving. I replied, "Absolutely! Excellent idea." In years past, we've traveled to be with family members at Thanksgiving. Not this year.

I'm grateful for the good news that there are promising results from Pfizer and Moderna with their coronavirus vaccines. That flickering light of hope is encouraging in these otherwise less light and indeed darker days. I was also encouraged this week by an interview I saw Monday evening on the PBS NewsHour with Dr. Francis Collins, the director of the National Institutes of Health.

In speaking of the progress on the vaccines, and their submission to the Food and Drug Administration for review, Dr. Collins said, "The FDA career scientists are extremely experienced and hardworking. They are 24/7 going through all of the steps to make sure that what we have is just as safe and effective as the public expects."

In response to a question from anchor Judy Woodruff, regarding where we are as a country in dealing with COVID-19, Dr. Collins said:

> It's such a moment of dramatic contrasts; to have these encouraging results from vaccine trials, but to know that those are still months away for most of us. And to see, at the same time, this explosion of the pandemic across the country . . . This is what we all feared might happen when cold weather came in. So, wear the mask. This is not an invasion of your personal freedom. This is actually a lifesaving medical instrument. We have the data for that. With Thanksgiving coming and other holiday gatherings, I think we're all really concerned that this could get even worse if we don't follow the guidelines, the three W's: Wear your mask, watch your distance, and wash your hands. [1]

I never thought of my mask as a lifesaving medical instrument, but that's exactly what it is. Now more than ever, in order to be a good neighbor to you, I need to be mindful of what I'm doing and not doing. When Ms. Woodruff asked Dr. Collins if there was one message today for the American people, Dr. Collins didn't miss a beat:

> The cavalry is coming. The vaccines are working. Biotechnology and this hard work of industry, academia and the NIH, has paid off in a dramatically rapid fashion; we have never seen anything quite like it before. It usually takes eight years to get to this point. We did it in eleven months, and yet no corners were cut. So, be enthusiastic and excited and encouraged about that. We are also in a dark period here with this pandemic. It is up to all of us to further increase our attention to what we can do day

1. PBS NewsHour. Seattle: KCTS, Nov 16, 2020.

by day. Just like wearing a seat belt, put on your mask. It's a way to save lives. We can all do a better job of this if we just hang in there for a few more months. [2]

I've been an admirer of Dr. Collins for many years. Earlier this year, he was awarded the Templeton Prize for challenging the idea that science and religion are at odds. Dr. Collins is one of the most accomplished scientists in the country. He directed the Human Genome Project to completion, illuminating the genetic blueprint of the human species. As the NIH director, Dr. Collins oversees the federal government's biomedical and public health research efforts. In response to the Templeton Prize announcement on Twitter, Dr. Collins—who is a Christian—said he was "profoundly humbled" by the recognition. "The realization that principles of faith and science are complementary has been of great comfort to me in the search for truth."

In a statement released by the John Templeton Foundation, Dr. Collins was also quoted as saying:

> Almost my every waking moment is consumed by the effort to find treatments and a vaccine for Covid-19. I grieve at the suffering and death I see all around, and at times I confess I am assailed by doubts about how a loving God would permit such tragedies. But then I remember that the God who hung on the cross is intimately familiar with suffering. [3]

Dr. Collins told the *Religion News Service* that his faith has informed his response to the pandemic. Quoting Psalm 46, Dr. Collins said: "'God is our refuge and strength, an ever present help in trouble.' If we want to look at God's role in the coronavirus pandemic, that's where I'd look." [4]

In 1527, Martin Luther faced one of the greatest difficulties of his life as the Bubonic Plague swept across Germany and much

2. PBS NewsHour. Seattle: KCTS, Nov 16, 2020.

3. Templeton Prize Announcement, May 20, 2020.

4. Kathryn Post, "NIH Chief Francis Collins Wins Templeton Prize." *Religion News Service*, May 20, 2020.

of the European continent. According to Steven Lawson's "Luther and the Psalms: His Solace and Strength," Luther's son almost died and Luther's own body was fainting under the mounting pressure. Lawson writes:

> In the midst of this personal conflict, Luther found himself contemplating the promises of Psalm 46 . . . Gaining new strength, Luther composed his most famous hymn, "A Mighty Fortress." Amid such adversity, Luther found God to be a 'bulwark never failing.' Many times during this dark and tumultuous period, when terribly discouraged, Luther would turn to his co-worker, Philipp Melanchthon and say, 'Come, Philip, let us sing the 46th Psalm.' Together they would sing it in Luther's original version: "A sure stronghold our God is he, a timely shield and weapon; our help he will be and set us free from every ill can happen."[5]

5. *Lawson,* Preaching the Psalms.

My 2020 Christmas Playlist

December 4, 2020

My heart is steadfast, O God . . . I will sing and make
melody. (Psalm 57:7)

BETWEEN WRITING THE TITLE OF today's pastoral letter and composing this sentence, a United Parcel Service driver knocked on the front door notifying us of a delivery: a beautiful Christmas wreath, the gift of friends who've been providing us with our front door Christmas wreaths for years. Still, the Christmas cards are sitting on a shelf; we haven't written or addressed them yet. Our Christmas decorations are in their boxes in a closet, as we haven't purchased our Christmas tree yet. In other words, we've got some Christmas preparations to do. Thankfully, there is one Christmas tradition I can check off my to do list: my 2020 Christmas Playlist is done.

Curating an annual Christmas playlist is one of my favorite Advent projects. For the most part the songs on my playlist are Advent/Christmas-focused. The playlist reflects my eclectic musical tastes: I love jazz, folk, blues, country, bluegrass, rock 'n' roll and just about every other genre of music. Some of these songs are traditional, re-arranged Christmas carols, while others are originals; all of them are songs I love. They brighten my days and cheer my soul. If I could, I'd burn each and everyone of you a copy of my

2020 Christmas Playlist, but I can't (iTunes won't permit it). So, here's the next best thing: My (annotated) 20-song 2020 Christmas playlist:

1. "Christ the Lord is Born" by Sufjan Stevens, is a lovely solo piano prelude.

2. "Oh, Mary and the Baby, Sweet Lamb" by Elizabeth Mitchell, is a lively chorus with flute, handclapping, drumming, a soloist and young voices announcing the birth of Mary's baby, "sweet lamb."

3. "Snow" by Sam Baker. Mr. Baker is a Texas based singer-songwriter. Accompanied by solo piano, guitar, and cello, "Snow" revels in the sights, sounds, and musings of the narrator/observer on a wintry morning in Boston.

4. "Come Thou Long Expected Jesus" by Bill Mallonee, is a lean and winsome arrangement of the traditional carol. Mr. Mallonee, founder of "Vigilantes of Love," sings his heart out as he celebrates Jesus, "the joy of every longing heart."

5. "Carry Me Home" by Hey Rosetta, a Canadian based band led by singer songwriter Tim Baker, is a prayer—a plea—for help to get home.

6. "Once in Royal David's City" by Los Angeles based folksinger Claire Holley, is a lovely arrangement of the traditional carol bearing witness to the gracious gift of the incarnation.

7. "Shut in at Christmas" by Kelly Willis and Bruce Robison is as sweet a version of this country Christmas song, written by Ira and Charlie Louvin, as you'll ever find. The website, "Hip Christmas" considers this song "maudlin." Though there is a whiff of self-pity, it's a perfect sheltering-in-place 2020 Christmas song, a gentle reminder that "the Savior won't forsake me."

8. "Baby King" by John Cowan, is a soulful, funky bluegrass celebration of Jesus, the baby king. Originally written and recorded by Jesse Winchester, I love this cover.

9. "O Come, O Come Emmanuel" by Rosie Thomas, is beautiful. It's my favorite version of this beloved Advent hymn inspired by Isa 7:14: "Therefore the Lord himself will give you a sign. Look the young woman is with child and shall bear a son, and shall name him Emmanuel." Ms. Thomas's voice perfectly reflects the yearning and longing of the words and the melody of this ancient carol.

10. "Peace" by Michael McDonald was written by McDonald and Beth Nielsen Chapman. In his liner notes, Mr. McDonald writes that the album on which it appears, *In the Spirit: A Christmas Album*, is dedicated to "everyone who seeks to understand God's love for us." It's a perfect Christmas prayer.

11. "Getting Ready for Christmas Day" by Paul Simon, rocks and rolls and dips and soars. Written by Paul Simon with samplings from a sermon by the Rev. J.M. Gates, this is an Advent lament tinged with Christmas hope.

12. "Refugee King" by Liz Vice (featuring Hannah Glavor) was inspired by the account of the flight into Egypt (Matt 2:13–15.) Ms. Vice's post-Christmas song reminds me of the Psalms of Lament as she soberly sings of the wickedness of the world's powers and principalities while trusting in the abiding presence of Jesus.

13. "Joy to the World" by Vanessa Williams and Brian McKnight is a soulful, brassy wonder. While this arrangement may not be everyone's cup of Christmas tea, the carol is after all about the joy the savior brings, not to mention the wonders of his love. I find this rousing rendition of "Joy to the World," to be gloriously exuberant!

14. "Away in A Manger" by Philip Aaberg, a Montana based solo pianist, is a selection from his album, *Christmas*. The simple elegance of Mr. Aaberg's artistry is timeless. In his liner notes, Mr. Aaberg writes that he recorded the album "in the hours between midnight and 4:00 am in December of 2000 while I awaited the birth of my son." His "Away in the Manger" is a lilting lullaby.

15. "Angels We Have Heard on High" by Mike Schmid is a lean and simple version of this beloved carol. While I'm accustomed to bigger and brassier arrangements of this song, I have come to appreciate the quiet beauty of Mr. Schmid's voice and his light touch on the piano. The keyboardist for Miley Cyrus and The Chainsmokers, Mr. Schmid's recording of this Christmas standard is pretty different from his usual gigs.

16. "Some Children See Him" by Sixpence None the Richer, is my (current) favorite version of a carol composed in 1951 by Alfred Burt and and Wilha Hutson. The poetry of the carol's inclusive celebration of the incarnation is as gracious as can be.

17. "The First Noel" by The David Crowder Band is a musical Christmas card: shepherds, angels, the star and wise men all invite us to join the angelic chorus: "Noel, Noel, Noel, Noel." Mr. Crowder, a great rock 'n' roller, mostly keeps the lid on the band as they slowly build musical momentum, ending with ringing guitars singing glory in the highest. Yes!

18. "In the Bleak Midwinter" by Jerry Douglas, is an instrumental version of the carol by Christina Rossetti and Gustaf Holst. Mr. Douglas's dobro perfectly captures the haunting poignancy of this wintry and down to earth Christmas offering.

19. "Joy" by Whitney Houston and the Georgia Mass Choir from the soundtrack of the 1996 film, "The Preacher's Wife," is a jubilant and exhilarating celebration of the gift of Christmas. When Ms. Houston sings, my soul is heartened, uplifted, and blessed.

20. "Silent Night" by Bela Fleck and the Flecktones, is a jazzy, jingle-jangle not so silent arrangement of the most beloved Christmas carol of all time. Bela Fleck's banjo, Victor Wooten's bass, Future Man's percussion and Jeff Coffin's woodwinds, band together offering up a spirited and upbeat performance. It's not so calm, but it sure is bright, as the musicians revel in the dawn of redeeming grace.

Abundant Life

Thursday, December 10, 2020

I have come that you may have life, and have it abundantly.
(John 10:10)

I WAS SITTING IN THE spacious living room of a big ranch house in Woodland Hills, California, about a mile or two from the campus of Los Angeles Pierce Junior College where I was a first year student. I was attending my first meeting of Campus Crusade for Christ and the speaker, Bob Kraning, was talking about Jesus. Mr. Kraning talked about how Jesus *was* our savior, no doubt about it, but he was also our Lord. He asked us if Jesus was the Lord of our lives. To be honest, I'd never given it much of a thought.

The talk Bob Kraning gave that day was a turning point in my life. I'd been a Christian since I was baptized when I was eight years old but I'd never thought of myself as a disciple of Jesus, or that Jesus was my lord. Though I couldn't have articulated it at the time what I knew was that I wanted to follow Jesus and live my life in a way that was pleasing to God.

I wanted to follow Jesus and I wanted to live the abundant life Jesus said people could live if they followed him. I have lost my way more times than I can count. The problem is that my desire to follow Jesus is undermined by my sinful self. Campus Crusade's little booklet, *The Four Spiritual Laws* (written by Bill Bright) said that my sin was the thing that stood between me and living the abundant life. That made sense to me.

What's the abundant life? It's a life lived for God and others. Jesus said, "If you want to find your life you'll lose it, but if you lose your life for my sake, you'll find it" (Matt 10:39). An abundant life is not necessarily a great big life. Your abundantly lived life may not get your name in lights or garner you a Nobel Peace Prize, but it's a life worth living just the same. A genuinely abundant life is a life lived for others.

Over the years, novels have played a pivotal role in helping me understand what it means to follow Jesus. *Mr. Blue* by Miles Connolly; *The Last Western* by Thomas Klise, *Mariette in Ecstasy* by Ron Hansen, *Gilead* by Marilynne Robinson, *Screwtape Letters* by C.S. Lewis and *The Hammer of God,* by Bo Giertz, have all been instrumental in teaching me the many and varied ways following Jesus inspires and empowers people for abundant life.

The Last Year of the War by Shirley Nelson is another one. Her novel is set at the Calvary Bible Institute in Chicago in the last year of World War II, where Jo Fuller, a born-again Christian and first year student wrestles with one surprise after another. Nothing and no one is what she expected. My favorite part of the novel is a chapel sermon preached by Dr. Peckham. His message is a bracing, engaging and grace-centered proclamation of abundant life.

> Jo sat with her notebook and pencil feeling hopeful. Dr. Peckham began by saying he had been getting a lot of questions about something called the "victorious life," or "the life that wins." He had been asked if he believed in such an experience, and his answer was yes, he did, but if he must name it he would rather call it, "the life that loses." As I get the picture, the life that wins is a shining life in which we are endowed moment by moment with unquenchable joy and a new strength of character. We want to be like Christ, we say. We want to have His heart … to be courageous, serene in the face of adversity, powerful in soul-winning, steady and unmovable in faith, free from the tyranny of self, flesh crucified, all in our places, with sunshiny faces.

But friends, it may not go that way. If you ask for the heart of Christ, yours may be broken. If you ask for the eyes of Christ, you may be horrified at what you see. If you try to embrace all humankind, as Christ did, you may be consumed by that love. Touching broken lives means to be touched back by the world's misery. The healer risks infection . . . If we fight injustice, we are identified with the condemned. We will bear about in our bodies the paradoxes of humanity, the yeas and nays.

To be a Christian in the truest sense may mean to live on the edge of a cliff, shocked and dismayed at our own weakness, failure and evil. We go there as pilgrims and pioneers and only God can keep us safe on that wild frontier. If we understand all that when we talk about the abundant life, then we are ready for business.

But do I mean we should give ourselves to a life of sorrow and sackcloth, or sit looking for trouble, or that you should not be lighthearted and young? Of course not. Christ said, "My joy I give unto you." We mount up with wings as eagles. The fruits of the Spirit are joy and peace. What we have then is a flat contradiction. Dead in him; alive in him. "As dying and behold we live; as chastened and not killed; as sorrowful, yet always rejoicing; as poor yet making many rich; as having nothing, yet possessing all things." That's the life that wins. [1]

---

1. Nelson, *Last Year of the War.* 202–203.

Don't Fret. Joy is Coming.
December 17, 2020

You have turned my mourning into dancing; you have
taken off my sackcloth and clothed me with joy, so that
my soul may praise you and not be silent. O Lord my
God, I will give thanks to you forever. (Ps 30:11–12)

THIS PAST SUNDAY MORNING, our Zoom adult class completed our
reading and discussion of Mark Yaconelli's bracing and powerful
book, *The Gift of Hard Things: Finding Grace in Unexpected Places.*
Talking about topics like burnout, disappointment, brokenness,
loss, and suffering, might not seem like a great way to begin a
Sunday morning but it was. Our conversations were honest, in-
sightful, and surprisingly hopeful. What is striking about the
book is that for the author, each one of these difficult subjects was
prefaced by the word "gift"—as in the *gift* of burnout, the *gift* of
brokenness, and the *gift* of disappointment.

At a rest stop off I-5 in southern Oregon, I stepped out of the
car and noticed an old converted school bus across the parking lot.
There was a spray-painted banner hanging on the side of the bus
that read, "Anything is a Blessing." I took a photo of the banner
and every now and then I run across it and ponder the words and

their meaning. Anything is a blessing? Really? Anything? In the introduction to his book, Mr. Yaconelli writes:

> From Jesus' perspective our sufferings provide an opportunity for awareness, insight and enlightenment. In the Beatitudes (Matt 5:1–12) we hear Jesus claim that our disrupted plans, our broken faith, our poverty and sufferings, our grief and unmet longings can be held as gifts that make us more compassionate toward others and more open and available to God's love. [1]

It's been a difficult and daunting year: living through a global pandemic, with countless losses, disruptions, growing unemployment, a struggling economy, 300,000 deaths of our fellow citizens (a surreal number that staggers the imagination) a divided electorate, racial unrest, not to mention upended routines, students engaged in remote learning and parents working from home. In the face of all the changes we have endured, the constants have been God's faithfulness and promises: mercy, forgiveness, unconditional love, a hope that endures, and the assurance that no matter what we think or how we feel, God is with us.

As a congregation, SHLC has a lot to be grateful for thanks to the efforts of the church council and staff members whose commitment and resourcefulness have made it possible for the us to adapt to life together in spite of sheltering in place, lockdowns and quarantines. Thanks to technology we have been able to stay connected and worship, meet, work and learn together in spite of the fact that we cannot be *physically* together. The congregation's generosity has made it possible for Sammamish Hills Lutheran Church to sustain its mission and ministries. Thanks to the work of the call committee, the congregation will welcome new co-pastors Nyla and David Schoeld next month.

In a penetrating and sublime passage in *The Gift of Hard Things*, Mark Yaconelli writes about joy and loss:

> We come from joy, we return to joy. That is my authority as a spiritual guide, as flimsy as that may seem to the

---

1. Yaconelli, *The Gift of Hard Things*, 12–13.

world. It is my knowing and trusting and waiting for this joy that makes me a Christian. Not my seminary studies, not my resume, not my skills in counseling, or teaching or preaching; it is this secret, silent voice that says, "Don't fret. Joy is coming." Within my deepest loss and sorrow there persists real trust in life, in people, in God. Something in me waits patiently beneath the hurt and grief, confusion and pain, knowing that eventually I will discover peace. [2]

God's peace has been poured forth time and again as we have sought to be of loving service to God, each other and our neighbors in need.

Reading the last chapter of *The Gift of Hard Things* brought to mind Psalm 30. The psalmist's prayer testifies to God's faithfulness in spite of pain and suffering. "Weeping may linger for the night, but joy comes with the morning . . . You have turned my mourning into dancing; you have taken off my sackcloth and clothed me with joy, so that my soul may praise you and not be silent. O Lord my God, I will give thanks to you forever" (Ps 30:5b, 11–12). It's been a tough year. Vaccines are on the way. Don't fret—joy is coming.

Grateful for God's faithfulness, I thank God for each and every one of you, friends and members of Sammamish Hills Lutheran Church. Your prayers, your participation in our life together, your support of SHLC mission and ministries, and your gracious kindnesses have been a gift and blessing to me. Thanks!

2. Yaconelli, *The Gift of Hard Things*, 139.

Bibliography

Beresford, Bruce, director. *Tender Mercies*. 1983 United Kingdom: EMI Films. 1983.

Berry, Wendell. *New Collected Poems*. Berkeley, California: Counterpoint, 2012.

Buechner, Frederick. *Wishful Thinking: A Theological ABC*. New York, NY: Harper & Row, 1973.

Buechner, Frederick. *Beyond Words: Daily Readings in the ABC's of Faith*. San Francisco, CA: HarperCollins. 2004.

Bruner, Frederick Dale. *Matthew, A Commentary, Volume 1: The Christbook (Matthew 1–12)* Revised and Expanded Edition. Grand Rapids, MI: William B. Eerdmans, 2004.

Chittister, Joan, O.S.B. *The Rule of Benedict: Insights For The Ages*. New York, NY: The Crossroad, 1992.

Curry, Andrew. "Before the Fall." *The Wilson Quarterly* (Fall 2009). https://www.wilsonquarterly.com/quarterly/fall-2009-the-future-of-the-book/before-the-fall.

De Sales, Francis, and Jane de Chantal. *Letters of Spiritual Direction*. Translated by Peronne Marie Thibert, V.H.M. Mahwah, NJ: Paulist, 1988.

Dickinson, Amy. "Wife Does Not Want to Join Husband As He Makes His Way Back to Church." Ask Amy. Seattle, WA: *The Seattle Times*, August 2, 2020.

Evangelical Lutheran Worship. Minneapolis, MN: 2006.

Goldingay, John. *Psalms, Volume 3: Psalms 90–150*. Grand Rapids, MI: Baker Academic, 2008.

Grindeland, Sherry. "The Day The Klan Came To Town." *The Seattle Times* (July 25, 1997). https://archive.seattletimes.com/archive/?date=19970725&slug=2551338.

Grudin, Robert. *Time And The Art of Living*. San Francisco, CA: Harper & Row, 1982.

Guralnick, Peter. *Sam Phillips: The Man Who Invented Rock 'n' Roll*. New York, NY: Little, Brown, 2015.

Hansen, Ron. *Mariette in Ecstasy*. New York, NY: HarperCollins. 1991.

Hawks, Howard, director. *Ball of Fire*. Hollywood, CA: Samuel Goldwyn Productions. 1941.

Bibliography

Hoomans, Joel. "35,000 Decisions: The Great Choices of Strategic Leaders." *The Leading Edge* (March 20, 2015). https://go.roberts.edu/leadingedge/the-great-choices-of-strategic-leaders.

Hunter, Carl, director. *Sometimes, Always, Never.* Los Angeles, CA: Blue Fox Entertainment. 2018.

Illibagiza, Immaculee, with Steve Erwin. *Left to Tell: Discovering God Amidst the Rwandan Holocaust.* Carlsbad, CA: Hay House, Inc., 2006.

Jacobson, Rolf A., ed. *Crazy Talk: A Not-So-Stuffy Dictionary of Theological Terms.* Minneapolis, MN: Augsburg, 2008.

Lawson, Steven J. *Preaching the Psalms.* Darlington, County Durham, United Kingdom: Evangelical, 2014.

Luther, Martin. *Luther's Small Catechism,* Translated by Timothy J. Wengert. Minneapolis, MN: Augsburg Fortress, 2008.

Mayo Clinic. "Anger management: 10 tips to tame your temper." (February 29, 2020.) https://www.mayoclinic.org/healthy-lifestyle/adult-health/in-depth/anger-management/art-20045434.

Merton, Thomas. *Thoughts in Solitude.* New York, NY: Farrar, Straus and Giroux, 1999.

Moore, Charles E., ed. *Provocations: Spiritual Writings of Kierkegaard.* Walden, NY: Plough, 2002.

Nelson, Shirley. *The Last Year of the War.* Eugene, OR: Wipf and Stock, 2004.

Norris, Kathleen. *Amazing Grace: A Vocabulary of Faith.* New York, NY: Riverhead, 1998.

Palmer, Parker. "It's One of My Most Treasured Possessions." July 21, 2020. Greenville, South Carolina: The Center for Courage & Renewal.

Penner, Mike. "Goodwill Games: Score: U.S., 17, Soviet Union 0, Have Mercy: Baseball: As a Kind Gesture, The First International Tournament Game for the U.S.S.R is Halted After 6 ½ Innings." *The Los Angeles Times* (July 27, 1990). *https://www.latimes.com/archives/la-xpm-1990-07-27-sp-729-story.html.*

Peterson, Eugene H. *Christ Plays in Ten Thousand Places: A Conversation in Spiritual Theology.* Grand Rapids, MI: William B. Eerdmans, 2005.

————. "Listen Yahweh." *Christianity Today* (January 14, 1991). https://www.christianitytoday.com/ct/1991/january-14/listen-yahweh-elizabethan-rhythms-in-most-translations-of.html

Pingrey, Daniel. "A Message from Sammamish PD Chief of Police Dan Pingrey." City of Sammamish (June 2, 2020). https://www.sammamish.us/news-events/archived-newsid=55414.

Post, Kathryn. "NIH chief Francis Collins wins Templeton Prize." *Religion News Service* (May 20, 2020). https://religionnews.com/2020/05/20/francis-collins-nih-templeton-prize-winner-on-faith-and-coronavirus.

Smedes, Lewis B. *Love Within Limits: A Realist's View of 1 Corinthians 13.* Grand Rapids, MI: William B. Eerdmans, 1989.

Bibliography

Tayler, Jon. "30-3: Rangers and Orioles Players From MLB's Biggest Blowout Recall History-Making Game." *Sports Illustrated* (August 22, 2017). https://www.si.com/mlb/2017/08/22/30-3-texas-rangers-baltimore-orioles.

Taylor, W. David O. "Psalms of Justice." *The Gospel Coalition* (June 16, 2020). https://www.thegospelcoalition.org/article/psalms-of-justice.

Webbe, Gale. *The Night and Nothing*. San Francisco, CA: Harper & Row, 1964.

Wilkens, Carl H. *I'm Not Leaving*. Spokane, WA: Carl H. Wilkens, 2011.

Winner, Lauren F. *Wearing God: Clothing, Laughter, Fire, and Other Overlooked Ways of Meeting God*. Copyright © 2015 New York, NY: Harper One, 2015.

Woodruff, Judy. "Head of NIH Urges Americans To Take Precautions While Awaiting Vaccine." *NewsHour* (November 16, 2020). https://www.pbs.org/newshour/show/head-of-nih-urges-americans-to-take-precautions-while-awaiting-vaccine.

Wright, Tom. *Paul For Everyone, Romans Part 1: Chapters 1–8*. Louisville, Kentucky: Westminister John Knox, 2004.

Yaconelli, Mark. *The Gift of Hard Things: Finding Grace in Unexpected Places*. Downers Grove, IL: InterVarsity, 2016.

Zadra, Dan, and Kobi Yamada. *10: What's On Your Top 10 List?* Seattle, WA: Compendium, 2012.

CPSIA information can be obtained
at www.ICGtesting.com
Printed in the USA
FSHW022311281221
87251FS